Number 56
APPROACHES TO MODERN JUDAISM
Volume II

edited by
Marc Lee Raphael

APPROACHES TO MODERN JUDAISM
Volume II

APPROACHES TO MODERN JUDAISM
Volume II

edited by
Marc Lee Raphael

Scholars Press
Chico, California

APPROACHES TO MODERN JUDAISM
Volume II

edited by
Marc Lee Raphael

Library of Congress Cataloging in Publication Data
(Revised for vol. 2)
Main entry under title:

Approaches to modern Judaism.

(Brown Judaic studies ; no. 49, 56)
Includes bibliographical references and indexes.
1. Judaism—History—Modern period, 1750- —
Addresses, essays, lectures. 2. Judaism—United States—
Addresses, essays, lectures. I. Raphael, Marc Lee.
II. Series: Brown Judaic studies ; no. 49, etc.
BM195.A66   1983   296'.09'03   83-14202
ISBN 0-89130-647-1 (v. 1)
    0-89130-793-1 (v. 2)
    0-89130-794-X (v. 2 pbk)

Printed in the United States of America
on acid-free paper

For Marvin Zahniser

colleague, scholar, and friend

TABLE OF CONTENTS

PREFACE

The idea for APPROACHES TO MODERN JUDAISM came from Professor Jacob Neusner of Brown University who hoped that such a series would serve as a vehicle in three ways. First, it would enable colleagues to address methodological issues in various fields of modern Judaic Studies, especially by asking questions such as what is the most pressing issue in a given area? what have been the traditional ways of looking at these problems? and what might constitute a new approach? It might also stimulate, in various fields, non-methodological articles of substance. Finally, this series might generate fresh thinking about what constitutes modernity, and a discussion about the relationship between Judaism and various elements of modernity.

Laurence J. Silberstein's essay in methodology utilizes theoreticians outside the study of Judaism whose insights ought to help students of modern Judaism read and interpret texts. Silberstein describes some of the ways in which these scholars have shaped his own work in Jewish thought and, more specifically, his analysis of Martin Buber's writings.

William Cutter examines the ways in which students derive "meaning" from texts, and considers the effect of individual interpretation, community reading experience, and the authority of the academic tradition. He urges instructors to find pedagogical value in the occasional anarchies which different interpretive schools have promoted. Cutter appears to try to steer a middle ground between interpretive anarchy and normative readings of well-known texts.

Peggy Ward Corn brings fresh insight to D. M. Thomas' The White Hotel, a novel whose narratives which follow the heroine's erotic poem and journal attempt to explain the meaning of her life by interpreting her writing. Corn demonstrates how each successive interpretation subsumes the one before it by revealing its inadequacies, yet all the interpretations are essential in understanding the complexity of the heroine's multi-faceted identity. By means of this structure, Corn argues, Thomas makes it possible for modern readers to mourn the death of his heroine and thereby to begin to comprehend the enormity of the loss of the millions of "white hotels" who perished in the Holocaust.

Jeffrey S. Gurock describes Jews who defined their Orthodoxy more as an institutional identification than as an

ix

all-encompassing belief and ritual system, and argues that such Jews constituted that denomination's "rank and file" until the present generation. Today, he points out, the Orthodox laity (particularly in major American cities) is far more committed to the observance of traditional practice without as within the precincts of the synagogue, while the older "rank and file" Orthodox Jew has been winnowed out of affiliation in present day Orthodox synagogues.

Daniel Jeremy Silver reflects upon the past three decades of Reform Judaism in the United States and discoveres a movement lacking ideological coherence. In addition, he ponders what is happening to Reform once the liberal political agenda it so enthusiastically affirmed begins to vanish, for theological incoherence, once sustained by political values, is more nakedly exposed when its supporters begin to lose faith in their traditional social and political values. Finally, Silver briefly suggests the starting point for a compelling new focus.

Richard G. Marks describes and discusses one particular experiment--Buddhists in Thailand studying Judaism with an American Jewish professor in a university program of comparative religion--in interpreting Judaism across complex cultural and linguistic differences. It describes what the students perceived in the Judaism of the standard American textboks and analyzes some of the features of Thai culture which shaped those perceptions, focusing upon the term "holy" as an especially revealing problem of interpretation. The central question posed is what "understanding" can mean, what it involves, intellectually and in a personal sense, in a cross-cultural context.

These volumes, of which this is the second, will appear as often as necessary. I am extremely grateful to The Ohio State University College of Humanities for providing the typing support and to Professor Jacob Neusner for making publication possible.

Marc Lee Raphael
September, 1984

TEXTUALISM, LITERARY THEORY AND THE MODERN
INTERPRETATION OF JUDAISM

Laurence J. Silberstein
Lehigh University

In Jewish studies, as in many other academic fields, the
assumption prevails that one can separate the methodological
or theoretical framework within which an inquiry is carried
out from the practical activity of the inquiry itself. This
assumption, I believe, is not tenable and must be laid to
rest. Our questions, our conceptual frameworks, our criteria
of selection, and our modes of discourse all shape the outcome
of our inquiry and determine the conclusions that we arrive
at. This position has been effectively stated by Robert Baird
in an essay published in 1975 devoted to methodological issues
in the study of religion.

> Choosing not to discuss methodology simply leaves the
> logic of one's procedure to chance. It means that one
> simply chooses not to analyze, in a logical manner, what
> questions he is asking of his material and chooses not to
> determine the limitations of such questions....Of course,
> if a community of "scholars" simply agree by common
> consent to stumble along together, there is little one can
> do about it.
>   (Robert D. Baird, "Postscript: Methodology, Theory
> and Explanation in the Study of Religion." Methodological
> Issues in the Study of Religion, ed. R. D. Baird, Chico,
> Cal.: New Horizons Press, 1975, 112).

By methodology, I do not mean the scholarly procedures
employed in analyzing and interpreting data. Instead, the
term refers to the "analysis of assumptions and logical
limitations of the method" (Baird, "Methodology," 112). As
Karl Popper and others have convincingly argued, all research
is "theory laden."[1] To ignore the methodological inquiry is
to ignore the intellectual presuppositions which shape the way
in which we define our fields of inquiry, select the relevant
data, determine the appropriate questions, and evaluate the
evidence.

In the field of Jewish Studies, issues of methodology are
rarely raised. Moreover, when raised, they generally refer to
the scholarly procedures utilized in a given field. Thus, one
frequently encounters people who ridicule all efforts to
explore methodology as a separate inquiry. The field of
Jewish Studies includes historians, philologists, literary
scholars, philosophers, archaeologists, linguists and others.
Their areas of expertise encompass diverse geographical and

cultural settings in different time periods. Scholars of Judaica, therefore, utilize diverse methods and approach their work with differing intellectual premises. Thus, it is more accurate to describe Jewish Studies as a "field-encompassing" field.[2]

Yet anyone seeking to make sense out of a text, regardless of his or her orientation, must confront certain questions such as "What activities and processes are involved in the act of reading and interpreting a text? What does it mean to claim that this is what this passage or texts means? Are we claiming that the meaning inheres in the text? What part do we, the interpreters, play in producing this meaning? To what extent does our situation determine the interpretation that we produce? Should our primary concern by the original writer's intention? To what extent is that intention recoverable? What conventions of reading are called for by different texts?"

Other pertinent questions include "How do we account for the fact that the same text generates diverse interpretations? Are we prepared to claim that only one interpretation is correct? How do we explain the existence of diverse interpretations? If we reject the pluralistic alternative, how do we determine the most correct or valid reading?"

As a non-specialist who has recently been introduced to the field of literary theory, it appears to me that a convincing case for the priority of theory has been made by such writers as Culler, Derrida, Eagelton, Bloom, Foucault, Barthes and others.[3] In their works, the specialist in Jewish Studies can find a rich mine of insights concerning the process of textual reading and interpretation. Along with many others, these writers have raised theoretical issues which no scholar whose work involves reading can afford to avoid.

Jonathan Culler is one writer who has made a major contribution to clarifying the theoretical issues involved in the reading, writing, and interpretation of texts. In a recent work, On Deconstruction, Culler argues that such diverse figures as De Saussure, Marx, Freud, Goffman, Lacan, Hegel, Nietzsche and Gadamer have all made significant contributions to a field that he calls "textual theory." To Culler, a text is "whatever is articulated by language." Thus, a more convenient designation for this body of writings is simply the name, "theory." People engaged in the discussion of theory do not simply aim at improving existing interpretations. Instead, they redescribe existing fields in a way that challenges conventional disciplinary boundaries.

> The words we allude to as "theory," are those that have had the power to make strange the familiar and to make readers conceive of their own thinking, behavior and institutions in new ways. (On Deconstruction, p. 9)

Although often employing familiar techniques of demonstration and argumentation, works of theory, according to Culler, derive their force from "the persuasive novelty of their redescriptions." Such works call into question the presuppositions with which we normally work, forcing us to rethink what we do in different frameworks or paradigms. Works of theory, Culler points out, possess a distinct vitality and creativity and hold far-reaching implications for the humanities in general.

Thus, Freud did not simply contribute to the ongoing development of psychology, he altered the way in which the field of psychology was perceived. Similarly, Nietzsche or Wittgenstein did not philosophize in the conventional way, but developed an entirely new conception of philosophizing. As a final example, people like Barthes or Derrida did not simply add to our understanding of literary works; they altered our understasnding of literary works; they altered our understanding of literary interpretation. Moreover, their ideas have been utilized to alter existing assumptions and shape new perspectives in a variety of fields and disciplines.

During the past three years, I have become increasingly convinced of the relevance of many of these theorists to my own teaching and writing. In particular, while working on a study of Buber's writings, their ideas have helped me to overcome major obstacles and to resolve basic problems of interpretation. Furthermore, these writings have suggested new and exciting ways to view the overall develoment of Judaism. In the following pages, I would like to describe some of the ways that the field of literary theory, in particular, can contribute to our own field of Jewish studies. Far from constituting a comprehensive theoretical position, these observations and reflections are intended as preliminary, and are offered as a stimulus to further discussion.

The philosophical framework for the approach that I am outlining has been suggested by Richard Rorty, a philosopher who sympathizes with much post-structuralist literary theory.

In his volumes Philosophy and the Mirror of Nature and
Consequences of Pragmatism, Rorty has raised issues relevant
to all who engage in the reading and interpretation of
texts.[4] In a provocative essay devoted to the philosophical
implications of Derrida, entitled "Philosophy as a Kind of
Writing," Rorty contrasts two fundamentally different ways of
thinking:

> There then are two ways of thinking about various things.
> I have drawn them up as reminders of the differences
> between a philosophical tradition which began, more or
> less with Kant, and one which began, more or less, with
> Hegel's Phenomenology. The first tradition thinks of
> truth as a vertical relationship between representations
> and that which is represented. The second tradition
> thinks of truth horizontally, as the culminating
> reinterpretation of our predecesors' reinterpretation....
> It is the difference between regarding truth, goodness and
> beauty as eternal objects which we try to locate and
> reveal, and regarding them as artifacts whose fundamental
> design we often have to alter. (Consequences of
> Pragmatism, 92)

According to Rorty, whether one is looking at physics,
philosophy, or Jewish studies, there are essentially two ways
of viewing any field. On the one hand, it can be seen as an
effort to reveal and describe a given object or reality by
uncovering the basic elements and patterns of that reality.
This activity is a progressive one in which subsequent
generations arrive at better and more accurate ways of
describing that reality. At any rate, the criterion for
evaluating any description or interpretation is the extent to
which it corresponds to the reality or object we are seeking
to describe.

On the other hand, one can view members of a field of
inquiry as participants in an ongoing conversation which,
itself, helps to constitute this reality. The participants in
this conversation, the members of a field, are not all talking
about a common object or "reality." Instead, they participate
in the conversation by interpreting and criticizing the
contributions of prior or contemporary participants.
According to this view, what we define as reality is, to a
large degree, constituted by the conversation. Consequently,
the outcomes of these conversations cannot be tested by
correspondence to an external reality. Instead, we evaluate
such contributions in terms of their ability to stimulate
further conversation, make us look at the issues in new and
creative ways, or satisfy whatever needs or motivations
brought us to engage in the conversation in the first place.

If we were to apply Rorty's model to Jewish studies, the outcome would read like this:

Here is one way to view Jewish thought and Jewish writing. There is a determinate, distinct and authoritative corpus of ideas, behavioral patterns, and institutional networks which we call Judaism. While these may undergo change and development, there is still a core or essence which we refer to as Judaism. Thus, one can distinguish between ideas, patterns of behavior or institutional arrangements that are authentically Jewish or "really" Jewish, and others that are not. To write about Judaism is to engage in the activity of locating, revealing, and describing these ideas, behavioral patterns or institutional networks. The test of all such descriptions is, or course, the extent to which they correspond to the reality or object that we call "Judaism."

Here is another way to look at Jewish thought. What we refer to as Judaism is simply the cumulative interpretations that have been formulated by many writers over a long period of time. According to this model, it makes absolutely no sense to talk about Judaism apart from our interpretations of it.[5] Accordingly, to write about Judaism is, as in earlier periods, to think, talk, teach and write about what is conventionally referred to as Judaism. In carrying on this activity, people utilize different paradigms, i.e., different presuppositions, categories, concepts, and modes of inquiry and evaluation. The validity of their interpretations is not determined by correspondence to an objective given, but by conventions, usually unstated, shared by a broad group of thinkers or scholars.

People who engage in the study of Judaism often hold contradictory views about what precisely is Judaism. Moreover, there is widespread disagreement, usually suppressed, about which methods and procedures constitute the best way to make Judaism intelligible. It is not that later thinkers or writers have discovered better or more accurate ways of talking about or describing Judaism in any absolute sense. It is simply that the ways in which we choose to talk about Judaism serve our purposes better and allow us to pursue better the answers to the particular questions that concern those in our historical situation and in our framework of meaning. What joins earlier and later thinkers to one another is not the fact that they all study or describe a common object, but that they participate in a common conversation.

According to the first view, one could say that Jeremiah, Rabbi Akiba, Maimonides, Moses de Leon, Franz Rosenzweig and Gershom Scholem were all engaged in clarifying the true nature or essence of an objective phenomenon or entity called Judaism. Despite the differences among them, they all share a common object, Judaism. Accordingly, the ultimate test of their writings is the extent to which their descriptions correspond to the preeexisting object, Judaism.

However, utilizing Rorty's second model, one would say that the concept, Judaism, has no meaning apart from the various efforts to discuss it. It is not as if there is some preexisting essence which people subsequently attempt to describe. Rather, Judaism is a dynamic concept which assumes different forms and meanings depending upon who is talking about it. Judaism as discussed by Jeremiah, an anachronism in itself, is not the same as Judaism discussed by Akiba. Nor is Judaism as discussed by either of these the same as that discussed by Maimonides in an Aristotelian framework, or Moses de Leon from a mystical perspective. To argue, as did one writer, that when all is said and done, they all share common ideas of God, Torah and Israel is really to beg the question.

Thus, to criticize a particualr position by saying "But that isn't Judaism" is untenable. All that one could say is, "That is not the way in which I prefer to carry on the Jewish conversation or the Jewish mode of life." Seen in this light, to write or talk about Judaism is not to engage in the effort to accurately discuss an objective entity, but rather to participate in an ongoing conversation.

In an effort to concretize these themes, I would like to discuss briefly the ways in which I have utilized some of them in my work on Buber. One of the aspects of Buber's writings that has elicited much scholarly criticism is his inter-pretation of Judaism, and, in particular, his interpretation of Hasidism. The conventional approach to Buber's interpretation of Judaism/Hasidism is to ask, as did Scholem and Shatz-Offenheimer, "Did he get it right?" Such an approach presupposes that there is a fixed, determinate reality which we call Hasidism, and that all interpretations can and must be evaluated according to the extent to which they correspond to this reality.[6]

What such an approach overlooks, however, is the manifold problems embedded in this premise. For example, how do we define the parameters of this reality? Upon what do we focus: the institutions, spiritual experiences, concepts,

forms of behavior and ritual, etc.? Moreover, in reading a
Jewish/Hasidic text, what presumptions do we make about the
acts of reading and interpretation. Does the language "stand
for" or "represent" a reality which we will uncover if we
decode it properly? What constitutes the core of this
reality? Ideas? Institutions? Patterns of behavior?
Myths? Symbols? Modes of being in the world?
Religious/Spiritual states? All of them?

If one views reading and interpretation as a mimetic,
progressive activity by which one seeks to uncover an
objective reality, then the test for Buber's or anyone else's
reading is "to what extent does it correspond to objective
givens." However, if one accepts the theory of revisionism
suggested by Rorty, and applied to literary theory by Harold
Bloom, then the question of objective givens really turns out
to be a question of "canons" or conventional
interpreatations. What are claimed as authoritative readings
are themselves interpretations, the outgrowth of structuration
or canonization.[7] Consequently, to evaluate a particular
interpretation or reading of Judaism by asking whether it is
correct or right, is to presume the existence of a canonized,
interpretation-free text. Yet this canonized version is,
itself, the product of interpretation. We are, therefore,
pitting one interpretation against another. Thus, all reading
is intertextual, and all reading is interpretation or
"misreading."[8]

According to this revisionist orientation, which has also
been applied to the history of science in Thomas Kuhn's
seminal work, The Structure of Scientific Revolutions, one no
longer chooses a reading in accordance with whether it is
"really Jewish" or corresponds to "authentic Judaism," but
rather in terms of how well it does what we seek to do.[9] As
Rorty has stated it:

> The strong textualist simply asks himself the same
> question about a text that the engineer or the physicist
> asks himself about a puzzling physical object: how shall
> I describe this in order to get it to do what I want?
> (Consequences, 153)

Thus, in comparing interpretations of a text, we have to
ask ourselves what we want the reading or interpreation to do,
to accomplish? Do we want it to adequately reflect the
so-called literal meaning of the Biblical text? Do we want it
to preserve the structure of Talmudic Judaism? Do we want it
to reveal some deeper level of philosophical or moral truth?

Do we want it to reveal the mysteries of the godhead? Do we want it to contribute to a stable communal structure? Do we want it to bring the reader closer to a direct personal encounter with the divine? Do we wish it to help foster a socio-cultural milieu in which it is easier for people to relate to one another as I's to Thou's? Do we want it to strengthen the social and political foundations of a secular Jewish state? Do we want it to stimulate the creative imagination of the reader, thereby generating new texts and new interpretations?

According to Bloom, we should look at a text not as an object but, echoing the dynamic concept of the deconstructionists, as an event, a happening. When a poet writes, he does not create ab initio, but shapes his words in response to earlier poets. The act of creation, according to this view, is not a benign act, but one which results from conflict with a precursor. Moreover, any reading of the text is also an event. Consequently, a so-called interpretive text is no less an event than a work of interpretation:

> Your work as an event is no more or less privileged than the later poet's event of misprision in regard to the earlier poet. Therefore, the relation of the earlier to the later poet is exactly analogous to the relation of the later poet to yourself. (Kabbalah and Criticism, 63–64)[10]

The interpreter's reading of the text is no less an event than the text which we are reading. A text's claim to priority is not a given, nor is it something that is inherent in the nature of things (Kabbalah, 96–100). What we declare to be authoritative results from a decision to canonize particular texts. The authority of this canonization is as strong or as weak as the power of those who carry it out. Accordingly, in Bloom's interpretation, the later work is no less original than the earlier one. Thus, any sense of belatedness falls away.

Moreover, meaning arises not through isolated texts, but through texts in relationship to one another. Accordingly, a text is a relational event. As the structuralists understood, all texts have to be read intertextually.[11]

> There are no right readings, because reading is necessarily the reading of a whole system of texts, and meaning is always wandering around between texts. (Kabbalah, 107–108; cf. pp. 88ff.)

The categories introduced by Rorty and Bloom help to clarify the recurring question of whether a particular work is "really Jewish," a question often asked of such writers as Kafka. As Bloom has effectively argued, insofar as Freud and Kafka have shaped the way in which modern Jews read and interpret texts, they have had a strong impact on Jewish culture. Moreover, to the extent that Freud and Kafka participate in the Jewish conversation, they are an important part of Jewish culture. Thus, rather than utilize such vague categories as "commitment to perpetuating Judaism" or "intentionality," perhaps we should rephrase the question to read, "What impact do Freud and/or Kafka have on the modern Jew's ability to make sense out of his or her situation qua Jew, or of the condition of Jewish culture?" I.e., we translate the question from categories of "being" into categories of "doing," from states to happenings.

Another implication of the theories of Rorty and Bloom concerns the question of "influence." Conventional theories of influence seek to determine the extent to which ideas, forms, symbols, and patterns of behavior are faithfully transmitted from one reader to another. To what extent has B faithfully replicated and transmitted the ideas of A? To what extent are the ideas that are found in B the result of the influence of A? However, Bloom, drawing on Emerson and Nietzsche, argues that benign transmission does not make for strong, original or creative thinkers. The thinkers and writers who have the greatest impact are those who introduce new, creative, imaginative readings that diverge from the conventional and accepted. The writers whom we continue to read are not those who preserve, transmit or influence, but those who revise. Whether we are talking of the Yahwist, or Isaiah, or Rabbi Yehuda HaNasi, or Maimonides, or Moses de Leon, or the Besht, the test of the strong writer is originality.

What Bloom refers to as a "strong reading" does not disclose some hidden meaning inhering in the text, nor does it replicate a previous reading. Instead, it generates new meanings and introduces categories which subsequent generations, for various reasons, find useful. Thus, the Lurianic version of creation is powerful not because it is the most faithful rendering of the Biblical text, but because it provides a theodicy and a spiritual power that generates new creative energies which find their expression in Hasidism. If someone were to criticize Luria or Maimonides or Moses de Leon or Rav or Shmuel for either misreading the Biblical text or deviating from the intention of the author, most of us would find such a criticism ludicrous.

Similarly, when approaching modern interpreters like Buber, Kaplan, Heschel, Ahad Haam, or Rosenzweig, the criticism of "deviation from faithful mimesis" is also beside the point. Since all reading is interpretation, or, in the highly provocative phrase of the deconstructionists, "misreading," the question simply becomes, as Culler points out, which misreading is the acceptable one, and why![12]

Thus, when approaching a text, the revisionist thinks in terms of creativity and imagination, rather than continuity and benign transmission. Viewed in this light, strong readings emerge not in continuity with a precursor, but in conflict with him. As another contemporary critic, Edward Said, has written: "One doesn't just write; one writes against, or in opposition to, or in some dialectical relationship with other writers or writing." (Diacritics, v. 3 Fall, 1977, 35).

Thus, in the light of Rorty and Bloom, assisted by Wittgenstein, Dewey, Nietzsche, Freud and Emerson, I do not ask the extent to which Buber is faithful to a given tradition or the extent to which he has preserved and continued a tradition or whose ideas are reflected in his writings. Instead, I am led to a different set of questions:

1.   Rather than ask, "Who influenced him?" in the conventional sense of benign transmission, I ask, "Against whom or what was he struggling? Who were the precursors against whom he struggled in order to establish his meaning?"

2.   Rather than ask, "How faithfully did he replicate earlier writings and ideas?" I ask, "How did he misread and revise previous texts/ideas? What original interpretations did he offer?" It is not that the first question is wrong, it is simply that it is misplaced.[13]

3.   Viewing Buber's texts/readings as events, I am led, when reading a given text, to ask, "What was he doing? What kind of an activity was he carrying out?" Looking at the text I ask, "What does it do and how does it do it?"

As a result, I have come to view Buber's Hasidic tales as attempts to renew Jewish mythos and to repair the severed bond between the sacred and the human. Read in this way, his faithfulness to the received text is beside the point. Similarly, I read I and Thou as an attempt to alter conventional categories, concepts and, ultimately, modes of being in the world and modes of relating.

4. Finally, in order to evaluate Buber's own influence, I ask, "To what extent do the categories and ways of reading that he introduced meet the needs of subsequent readers and shape the way that they read and talk about Judaism?"

The revisionist replaces categories like "authority," "tradition," "canon," or "influence" by such categories as "originality," "event," and "defensive stance." In contrast to an Aristotelian, Hegelian, Platonic, or Darwinian paradigm, the revisionist uses a gnostic/kabbalistic paradigm. The question is never "Should we use a paradigm?" but rather, "Which paradigm shall we employ?" (Kabbalah, 86ff).[14]

Critics of the orientation advocated here often raise the charge of "anarchism."[15] "If," it is suggested, "no reading can make the claim to absolute validity, how can it be claimed that one reading is preferable toanother?" In my own work, for example, one could ask, "Why should one bother to consult this interpretation? How can one possibly test its value? What makes this reading better than that of a student virtually unfamiliar with Buber's works?"

To begin with, I do not claim that mine is "the" correct reading of Buber. Instead, I seek to shed new light on Buber's thought, and to offer interpretations that the reader will find provocative and suggestive. Moreover, in the final analysis, I hope that my interpretation enhances the reader's understanding of the dynamics of modern Jewish thought. Finally, I am hopeful that the reader of Buber may come away from future readings of Buber with a heightened self-awareness as an individual and/or as a Jew.

At the same time, in accordance with the canons of textual interpretation, I must substantiate my reading through a careful analysis of Buber's texts in relation to his other works and to those of his precursors. This, or course, does not preclude other interpretations. However, all interpreters, regardless of orientation, are expected to justify their readings through a careful analysis of texts. In evaluating any interpretation, I ask, "Has it provided a way of reading Buber that offers new insights and sheds new light on his thought? Does it clarify the nature of Buber's intellectual activity? Have its claims been substantiated by textual evidence, or, where this is not possible, by sound argumentation?"

I readily admit that my categories have no claim to
exclusivity. Other readers, utilizing other frameworks of
interpretation, may yield different interpretations that are
no less valid. Thus, to take one example, a Freudian may
produce a very different interpretation than the one that I
offer. Such an interpretation, rooted in a different set of
premises, could certainly yield valuable insights. Or, to
take another example, one could approach Buber's works through
the history of philosophy, seeking to situate him against the
background of Kant, Hegel, Kierkegaard and Feuerbach, among
others. While I might not find this approach the most
illuminating to my concerns, I certainly do not deny it an
appropriate place in the field of Buber scholarship.
Ultimately, much depends on why it is that one wishes to read
Buber in the first place.

In conclusion, I would like to return to the point from
which this essay began: the plea for theory. Theory, or
methodology--i.e., the systematic reflection upon the
premises, presupposition, categories and modes of inquiry that
we utilize--is not a luxury to which we retreat when we tire
of our "real" scholarly work. All that we do is "theory
laden." Consequently, theoretical discussion is essential to
our entire scholarly enterprise. To refer once again to Baird
whom I quoted at the outset:

> One cannot study anything without using some procedures or
> other. However, not all scholars have attended to
> methodology, that is, to the analysis of the logic of
> their method, its limits, and how it relates or does not
> relate to other methods. Some scholars simply stumble
> through their material without caring to articulate
> exactly what they are doing. Some stumble more skillfully
> than others. Choosing not to discuss methodology simply
> leaves the logic of one's procedures to chance. It means
> that one simply chooses not to analyze in a logical manner
> what questions he is asking of his material and chooses
> not to determine the limitations of such questions.
> (Baird, "Methodology," in Methodological Issues, 112)

MY TEXT, YOUR TEXT, OUR TEXT:
TAMING INTERPRETATIONS

William Cutter
Hebrew Union College, Los Angeles

This paper celebrates the fact that reading texts and
thinking about words are more important for intellectual life
than many anxious commentators had anticipated. Some students
of Marshal McLuhan, some contemporary educators like Neil
Postman,[1] and scores of educationists in the school domain
watch vigilantly the erosion of reading because of the
pervasive presences of television and computer capability. In
fact, both because of and in spite of technological
influences, interest in texts has come to reaffirm the
importance of the printed word and its meaning. The romance
with religious texts is pretty well established within many
contemporary communities, and adherents have actively argued
the value of finding meanings of their own.

But within Jewish scholarship there have been two
offshoots of the romance: one intellectual trend has tried to
demonstrate the indeterminacy of most material, including
religious texts; while another impulse of this romance is the
notion that we perpetuate the texts precisely because of the
determinacy, because of the enduring and univocal value
systems within them. This latter view is implied in the way
most Judaica courses are organized, and the view dominates
much of canonical scholarship. The adherents of the more
elastic view seek a license which, while potentially anarchic,
is actually committed to coherence as it reaches for different
kinds of "meanings."[2]

This tension between values and textual meaning has
captured my imaginmation for some time and is the subject of
this paper. And while we probably cannot resolve the tension,
my paper is part of a larger effort to understand it. Part of
our task will be to suggest some ideas about future thinking
and teaching. A premise of this paper is that from a
teacher's perspective a text with multivocal possibilities may
be seen as an opportunity for more realistic instruction
rather than a challenge to objectivity, though from the point
of view of "canon," a more cautious position is called for, as
I discuss below.[3]

Two metaphors have been particularly suggestive in
developing this work: one out of the personal experience of
nearly every parent; and the other from an image in one of
Nachman of Bratzlav's stories.

The first is the figure of a child in a museum, whom we have taken there because we anticipate what the child will acquire in the visit. That is, we have an idea that the museum will impart something specific, and that idea directs the way in which we organize our visit. But what actually happens is that if we leave the child alone for a moment, he begins to wander.

While we are following a pattern which conforms to our own intention in making the visit, the child has drifted to a dozen locations within the various galleries, and lighted here and there when something grabbed his eye. We may find him in front of a sculpture of an old man fishing, or an old woman baking bread. In each sculpture, a small child is at the foot of an adult. Apparently the young child identifies with the sculpture. Perhaps he likes bread? Or is fishing of special interest to him? It is possible that an image of a grandparent in the child's life or memory is evoked by the older figure in the sculpture. Our imaginary child is attracted to something in the statue, and seems willing to spend time in front of that figure, or with other figures in this exhibition room in hopes that others like it will be found. We, the parents, are now at a crossroads. We may stay with the youngster and gently coax him back into the more conventional routine of the museum; we may try to understand what interests him so that we might delicately weave his interests into what is the apparent purpose of the exhibit; or we may leave the child there, perhaps point out a thing or two, and then let him go to another location in the museum, creating his own experience entirely. And these are not our only choices. We could combine elements of each of them, either because we know that the original purpose in our visit is worth serving, or perhaps even because we need to establish our authority as the monitor of the visit. Sometimes we might do one thing and sometimes another. It would not help us here to judge which strategy is "best." But it is clear that this kind of thing does happen, and we who are parents and teachers often have to decide what to do when a student or child develops an interest in material which is not important to us, or responds to something in important material which was not the reason for our choosing that material in the first place. In the teaching of textual material, in visits to sites or museums, in the use of stories to emphasize moral points or patterns with the young, we are always faced with multiple layers of response. In some of our teaching and in some of our parenting we can ignore this fact, but in the reading of texts, the implicaions of this pedagogical reality should not be ignored. The fact is that most instructional design pays little attention to these implications.

In spite of the obvious differences between a museum experience and the experience of reading text, a number of similarities may be salient. In both experiences different things interest different people at different times, in spite of the fact that someone chose the text or the museum for a specific reason. The museum may have a fine selecton of women's art, and thus one parent may be inclined to go there frequently; it may have excellent installations which depict the history of subjects developmentally, and thus a parent with a pedagogical bent may be attracted to that scheme; it may have excellent viewing perspectives in comfortable surroundings. Or it may be near our homes. A body of texts may also inspire an instructor for a variety of reasons. Its basic philosophical outlook may interest the teacher. She may know the provenance of one body of material better than any other and thus feel comfortable presenting material from within that body. It may be organized in such a way as to enable students to learn efficiently on their own, or it may be related to a variety of interests in the students' current lives. It may also be accessible in the bookstore or the library. If this discussion sounds like a complication to the problem of canon, that is not entirely unintended. In any event, the teacher or parent or host may himself have developed some private intentions in planning the museum tour or the selection of texts as he did. In other words, she may have developed some private meanings of her own. The development of canon has always involved some subjectivity, probably more than we admit.

So much for the reasons we choose material for presenation to someone else. Clearly there are issues of canon; there are issues of convenience; and there are issues of intellectual affinity involved whenever we draw someone else into a cultural or academic experience. But it is equally clear that the person for whom we have developed these experiences may wander off into his own meanings. This paper deals with that wandering, since all places or pages have many possibilities, many contours and many meanings. But how do we know if any one of our many meanings is appropriate? What are the limits on our freedom? Is our sense of the text appropriate to its genre? And what conventions are used?[4]

In order to examine the issue of multiple meanings, we shall have to take into consideration a body of theoretical material which focuses on reader perspective and which has become increasingly important within the last decade and a half. I want to introduce this theoretical material with a pericope from the story of the Seven Beggars. It is found within the fourth tale of the major story by Nachman of Bratzlav (1772-1811), and it captures a paradox of profound theological impulse as well as a notion about the process of reading.[5] At the end of the world is its heart, a bit languid in the sun but ready to beat if properly inspired by its vision of a fountain which rests on a plateau at the top of a mountain at the other end of the world. The sight of the refreshing fountain impels the heart to move closer, and because longing stimulates the beating of the heart, it moves forward. But optical angles make it impossible for the heart to see the fountain as it moves closer, so that when the line of sight is broken, stimulation ceases. The beating stops. The heart must slip far enough backwards to see the fountain again so that the longing will recur and the beating resume. Thus, the longing is partially an end in itself.

My first scenario is an image of method, and my second one is an image of meaning. The two are related because at the core of teaching lies a concern with determining the meaning of material, and the material is selected because of meanings which reside in the material but which may not be important for the student. The distance between private and public understanding of texts, between the official meaning of a text and the way in which the text is translated is bridged by teaching methods. There is, at the same time, a suggestion that lack of closure (fulfillment) is a value, and this lack of fulfillment prompts a longing to know and understand. This is the search for meaning which we hear so much of today, or the less dramatic expressions of polysemiousness discussed in the work of Geoffrey Hartman[6] and Roland Barthes[7], who in turn make it possible for Georges Poulet[8] to speak of the power of the reader. The lack of closure, and hence satisfaction, is what propels us to study a text more than once. We repeat our reading to find new meanings or more satisfying ones. Yet, as E.D. Hirsch remarks, if we did not have a sense of conventional meaning, we would have no reason to believe that the text is important, nor a reason to insist that our students read it.[9] We are caught between a sense of meaning and an anxiety from not being certain what the meaning is. And this anxiety stimulates the development of primary and secondary meanings and even incorrect and correct meanings. Because of that uncertainty, we are always able to rediscover the meaning. In other words, we are always open to restimulation by the promise of closure or union with the "fountain".

Hirsch and others have found language which tries to moderate the anxiety and which ought to be used as the discussion progresses. Hirsch adopts an earlier distinction between meaning (sinn) and significance (bedeutung) in order to distinguish objective and subjective interpretation.

Whether or not one appreciates this depiction of textual interpretation, it is an unavoidable fact that we must come to grips with multiple interpretations of texts. I am going to argue that the freedom of interpretation which the above paragraphs describe is to the benefit of the teacher, if not always to the benefit of the scholar who must search out purer meanings and original intentions.[10] When it comes to the use of texts, in fact, scholars and practical educators stand at two poles. Scholars search for objective meaning within texts already assumed to appeal (or be important) to readers. They are the texts of the canon. But educators have often had to take a text whose objective meanings are more or less acknowledged and try to give it subjective value, relevance or utility, thus moving it from the scholarly to the popular canon.

This tension calls upon us to examine our relationship to literary texts in a new way which violates many of the critical approaches of the early twentieth century, culminating in the New Criticism of the forties and fifties.[11] But the violation is much more comfortable to a contemporary school of literary thought which includes scholars such as Bloom, Hartman, and Culler in the United States; Iser and Poulet on the Continent; and the work of Jacques Derrida, whose extreme notions of deconstruction may threaten any normative notion of meaning. The examination of meanings from the more practical educators' point of view would find a strong ally in Norman Holland's inquiry about how readers--in fact--interpret material, no matter what we determine as the proper interpretation.[12]

A teacher may in fact find many ways to use these distinctions depending upon how commonly acknowledged is one particular meaning over another (some critics call this the "stability" of a text). If the basic meaning of a text, its pure sense, is more or less established through historical or contemporary consensus, then the distinction between personal or construed meaning and canonical meaning is clear. I have found increasingly that texts which are more equivocal require that the instructor must first assert one official reading which disciplines a student. Construed meanings are obviously much more difficult to control, since any reader may decide whimsically and privately that a literary unit reflects something which is part of his/her interior experience. What resides in the reader, in other words, resides in the reader; and we do not have the access to a reader that we have to a text which we may re-examine for the evidence. A teacher cannot control the private associations of a student, but the teacher can try to help the student develop the sense of relative distances between personal interpretation and more or less accepted meanings. The teacher can also help a student suspend subjective response while the meanings of the text are being drawn out.

Perhaps I have indicated sufficiently the nature of the problem. But I will repeat one critical point: the belief that discovery of original meaning of texts is problematic in the first place can be both a convenience for teachers who like to begin with the relevance of material and a challenge, since that tendency can lead to abuses which take a reader way beyond Hirsch's horizon of meaning, or any horizon at all.[13] Texts cannot "mean" everything, and even where they remind readers of everything, that reminder is not always the result of the text's interaction with the reader, but rather the reader's interaction with himself.

Because Jewish text reading is done in group settings of one kind or another, the discussion becomes more complex, and the strategies become more interesting. The reading of classical Jewish texts is most often done in the presence of other people with partners in a classroom or in semi-devotional settings such as synagogues or home-study groups.[14]

Since most of us teach in a kind of "community" of readers, attention to what goes on within that community of readers not only multiplies the complexities which I have hinted at above but also helps resolve the pedagogical problems. Community is some antidote to the learner's isolation introduced by electronic technological metaphors. What happens to readers as they work through Jewish texts as a community of readers? All of the following suggestions posit the existence of a small class of students, each student possessing the same literary text from the "canon" of Jewish literature, each student sharing with the others some common affiliation or institutional attachment and purpose.

Although the goals of this reading community may not be spelled out, they generally include at least 3 components: the understanding of the primary meaning of the material; the attachment of some personal relevance to that primary meaning; and the creation within the reader of some identification with the tradition. The reading activity is done in public by one student in the hearing of teacher and colleague. A wide range of implied goals may include some sense that the selection of that text has the effect of perpetuating it within the organization which supports the community as affiliates or trustees. Those who affiliate with any learning institution are the beneficiaries of the selection of material for the classrooms. In all the ways in which the institution touches lay leadership or those who affiliate as supporters, the materials treated in the classrooms of that institution become part of the communal life. This is that material which gets quoted in public address and which is cited in memorandums on children's reports of what went on in school today.

The following catalogue of events, however, derives from my own experience and study of what happens to a group of readers who gather to examine Jewish texts with a leader responsible for "teaching" that material. I have visited a number of classrooms--populated by students of varying ages-- and examined the results of two "research experiences" with reading communities.[15] In addition, of course, I have tried to examine my own classes in which my standing outside of the experience may be giving my students the benefit of two teachers for the price of one, or the handicap of having a teacher with divided attention.

1. As the instructor leads the class through a text towards normative meanings, the individual reader struggles with the text on both subjective and objective levels. As different objective meanings are suggested, subjective meanings shift. Examples are so numerous that it is difficult to choose one which illustrates this precisely, but a simple passage within the Passover Haggadah illustrates the idea. The rabbis have discussed the Exodus from Egypt until the time when the students arrive to annnounce that their teachers have talked through the night. "Teachers, it is time for morning

prayers," says one of the students. Now the connection
between the previous material and this passage has to do with
the zeal with which the Passover story is told. The previous
passage is quite clear in its encouragement that we read the
story and tell of it at length. If this "meaning" is
emphasized, then the private associations of the student who
is reading the text, the personal significance of the text, is
likely to have something to do with religious zeal. But it is
also possible that the instructor is more interested in the
notion that the passage was placed here as a signal of the
religious revolt which occurred during the end of the Roman
occupation. This emphasis is more likely to invite the
development of personal significance related to the historical
heroism of the Jewish people and of one's own part in that.
Or, since the text alludes to the special relationship between
disciples and teachers (after all, it is the students who
remind the teachers of their obligations), another set of
private associations can be evolved. In sum, the student's
private, subjective and construed meanings, the "significance"
of a text, is modified by the instructor's determination of
the more important "objective" meaning of the text.[16]

It should also be noted that the move from objective to
subjective importance (from meaning to significance), will be
affected by the reader's ability to extrapolate from specifics
and find structural parallels. Is the Akiba-Moses legend in
Menachot the case for the oral law or an antidote to the
tragedy of death?

In a liturgical example, we can see an instance of how the
significance of a text may rely almost exclusively on the
absence of an idea. Since the Jewish liturgy refers to God in
exclusively masculine terms, feminist readers derive a
powerful "significance" in the personal concern with the
feminine possibilities of God language. Here the absence of
meaning actually heightens the presence of an opposite
significance.

2. Individuals within the community of readers
experience different layers of (objective) meaning and
(subjective) significance in their colleagues and peers.
Different characters within the reading community become
figures who are to be contended with, just as (as we shall see
below) different characters within the textual material itself
become objects of confrontation. The personal relationships
between members of a reading group affect not only one's
relationship to a text but also the text's relationship to a

class. I have noted on several occasions that a group of text readers may develop a kind of group ethos, rebellious, anxious, punning, which spills over into the group's response to the textual material.

This group ethos often influences what material looms as most important to a group and determines the material to which the group returns when review or general discussion is being held. It will certainly influence interpretation.

3. Readers identify with different characters in a narrative depending upon the emphasis of the instructor, the particular personality of the reader or readers, and the particular setting in which the teaching takes place. At first blush, it seems that younger readers respond more readily to biographical emphasis than more sophisticated readers, because personal identificaion is a common activity of young readers. However, it is often the case that more mature readers approach a narrative in terms of how they might have solved the same problem which is being discussed within the narrative, and when this occurs, it certainly helps move the reader forward through the text. As suggested in the introduction to this paper, the instructor may have less control over the reader's response, since readers who tend to identify with characters in a narrative begin to take off in their own directions. If a character in a narrative appeals to a given reader for entirely private reasons, the central meaning of the text may only be secondary for that reader. The instructor, paradoxically, may serve a good purpose by stimulating biographical identification. Of course, the basic text and its primary meaning must harness the reader and force him or her to acknowledge the main points of the material. For example, I may love the rebellious nature of King Saul, and occasionally even cheer him on, but eventually I must accept the biblical text's judgement of him. This problem is not unlike what happens every time a loveable villain in a movie attracts our sympathy. The difference here is that Saul's melancholy and his misbehavior are part of a tragic perspective with which we might identify in part so that we might fully appreciate the complexity of the human condition. I am suggesting at this point that not enough is made of biographical correspondence in our classical materials, and that the use of biography--whether in bible, rabbinic literature, or more modern material--may be one of the ways in which a reader is engaged by the text.[17]

4. Once the reader has arrived freely at his or her own significances, preferences and sympathies, the existence of primary meanings and the original intentions of the author of the material harness the reader to the text. Thus, one of the activities which a reader engages in has to do with balancing one's own appreciation for the material with the intent of the author (in our homely example, in other words, enjoying one's own tour of the museum but returning to the intent of the exhibit's designers). Sometimes the harnessing involves a simple philological point, at other times, the discipline is a more controversial appeal to textual consistency, and yet other occasions might require the intructor's appeal to historical data. Within this harnessing, another phenomenon takes place, and this has to do with the relationship of the student to the teacher.

5. The leader of the reading community represents an authority who arbitrates textual meaning and creates a fixed point of interpretation which other members of the community may either accept or reject. This is more complicated than may at first appear. Of course, the teacher must have the "final say," and the teacher represents the conventional reading of the text. But in the case of many Jewish texts, Midrashic or medieval thought, for example, the conventional reading is itself a rejecton of a previous text. This is in turn complicated by the fact that the teacher is himself an interpreter who, having wrestled with the text, has come up with an analysis of that material which may well have rejected previous norms. My son recently suggested a useful definition of the word "interpretation" when I told him that Liberal Jews interpreted dietary restrictions in different ways. "Oh," he said, "then 'interpretation' means breaking the law!" The law, in the world of stylistics and exegesis, is the conventional meaning of a text, and it is constantly in the process of being "broken" as new significances are found, and especially when new meanings develop. Thus part of the activity of group reading is developing familiarity with breakers of norms and their methods. Discipline and rebellion are constantly challenging each other in the interpretive activity.

Each of these reading events has to do with relating the reader to some meaning within the text which relates in turn to some event in the outside world. Richard Lanham refers to this as looking through the text, through, that is, to something in the "real world" which is outside the text. The meaning of the text connects to the world as we know it. The next stage in this discussion, and the next series of reading events, has more to do with the qualities of the textual surface, its form and shape, and the basic values which are suggested by "textuality." It is what Lanham calls the looking "at" the text,[18] and part of Geoffrey Hartman's "learning how read".[19]

6. First among these events is that reading a work creates an investment in the importance of the work and possibly in the tradition which the text represents. The more laborious the reading (short of completely frustrating the reader), the more dear the investment, especially if the labor has to do with meaning and is not with mechanics or phonics. The notion that the struggle to master something creates a special attachment to it once it is mastered is not radical. This occurs in the performance of a piece of music as well as in the mastery of a particular piece of literary material. What is new here is the idea that this phenomenon of mastery is not fully exploited when it comes to Jewish texts, and too often textual material is chosen exclusively for its specific themes (relationship to the world outside of the text) and not enough for its technical problems and prospects, the rich hermeneutic possibilities of the form itself.

7. It is with regard to a sense of form, the poetics of the material, that Lanham's notion of looking "at" a text may be most obvious. In Jewish texts, homiletical materials have definite forms, legal arguments often have an aesthetic shape, and the selection of material (both in terms of form and content) may, as Neusner argues, communicate the world view of its authors.[20] Indeed, the history of Jewish literature is to a large extent the history of the development of new forms, themselves responses to cultural climates and changing social patterns, themselves a response to what is the priority in the society in which the Jew was functioning, and themselves symbolic (as in the case of Modern Hebrew Literature) of a rebellion against the norms of the culture which gave it birth. Thus, we can say that one important part of learning textual meaning has to do with exposure to ways of making meaning. Hermeneutic and exegetical devices expose the reader to different ways of drawing understanding from experience.

8. An additional version of concentration on textual form and the centrality of the text as a thing in itself comes from a combination of attention to the form-content nexus and memory of like texts. This occurs when we recall other texts

which relate--through form or content--to the core text with which we are dealing. In spite of the hermetic ways in which we may view a given text, there are always at least two ways to tie that text to a broader range of Jewish textuality: the mimetic mode, in which we recognize the way in which a given event or point relates to similar content in another text, and the formal level in which we recall a similar literary pattern or stylistic device. This intertextuality, the knitting of text to text and idea to idea, is often the hallmark of academic instruction, but Jewish teachers have not taken enough advantage of its potential. Whether we connect the poetry of moderns like Pagis or Tschernickowski to the classical literature, or the narrative material of Genesis to the philosophy of Maimonides, the tradition is so rich in intertextual associations that noting them seems superfluous. But the intertextuality occurs also on the formal level: legal and narrative formulations from one period which both attach themselves to and depart from earlier forms, early and late poetic forms which may demonstrate the changing power of the language, or the impact of informal "street" language on the development of the nation. And these connections also contribute to a sense of a total body of traditional literature arrived at not only through meanings, or through looking through a text to the world with which we are dealing, but looking "at" texts, in order to understand the full importance of literary form and the way in which narrative shapes our understading of the meaning of shapes.

9. As we near the end of the catalogue of reading events, we must once again focus on the reading activity itself. A reader engages in the act of looking for concealed meanings and in unravelling notions or words which are concealed.[21] The reader also engages in looking for meanings which he has identified already, but which he nonetheless enjoys rediscovering. The process whereby we repeat the ritualistic uncovering of what we know to be underneath explains the re-reading of a conventional text, the telling of a favorite joke or, in the domain of sacred ritual, the uncovering of the Torah.

If we had to summarize these reading events, we would have something like this: texts are polysemous (they have many meanings); some of these meanings are primary and some are secondary or even tertiary. If one pays attention to "what really goes on when people read," one gets a clearer sense of how both primary and secondary meanings influence what a reader draws from material. Some of what is drawn out is far removed from original meanings. Furthermore, the reading experience has a lot to do with what goes on "sociologically speaking," that is, the reader is the member of a reading community. Concentration on formal features of texts helps turn students into makers of meaning.

Students learn, in the process of group text reading, to hold alternate meanings at the same time, and they learn to connect the texts to other texts of like theme or structure. Students learn something about the place of form: the aesthetics and the structure of argument; and different techniques of interpretation which may influence the ways in which they will interpret all of their experience. They will do all of this in the context of a deveoping group spirit which both determines the derivation of meanings and influences the individual efforts at deriving personal significance. The student will also experience the personality of the group leader, the _moreh_, the authority, the transmitter of tradition. Each of these learnings is enhanced by sharing the experience through reading aloud.

On the one hand, then, we have a text which is always changing and a reading group which is audience, antagonist, and co-meaning-maker. On the other hand, we believe that there is a more or less conventional meaning to a text, a conventional reason for including that text within the canon, and a defined group of people who are ready to be taught the text, and whom we hope to invest with certain of our expectations.

A background to this summary might be helpful before we turn to some discussion of teaching method. This background is made up of three facts out of my own teaching experience: two which relate to the indeterminacy of text reading, and indeed all human experience; and one which relates to stability and universals. The first important fact is that material may be comprehended without being remembered, and material which is not compreheneded completely may often be precisely that material which is remembered for purposes of creative thinking. Learners often complain that they have not comprehended an idea and thus can do nothing with it, but teachers may find that it is precisely that material which can be returned to beneficially when building future discussion. The second item to note is that even relevance, that is, personal significance, may change--not only from person to

person as we would expect--but for any given person at
different times. These two points which connect us to the
dynamic nature of this enterprise are obviously connected with
the two images with which I opened this paper. But there is a
compelling third notion that represents a more stable pole in
this discussion. It is the fact that different instructors
have historically chosen similar materials for textual reading
even though their reasons might be entirely different. The
canon is remarkably constant, considering the varieties of
people who are doing the choosing and the varieties of
audience for whom the material is chosen. There seems to be a
certain universal latent in some material even when
instructors are not aware of it. Has one consistent notion
been advanced, for example, for the choosing of Pirke Avot as
a legitimate expression of the rabbinic tradition?

I am going to draw on the nine kinds of activities which
are the core of this paper and combine them with the three
premises which began this section. I propose that a
reasonable examination of these reading events, and of these
generalizations about the experience of reading and learning,
might guide us as teachers to focus on four elements which
serve as the "metasubject" of Jewish textual reading: First
is the notion of discovery of meaning as a basic Jewish
enterprise--both a theme and an activity of the classroom.
Second is the "strain" between any individual and the
tradition or study group. We might call this strain the
thematics of individual and community. Third is the
importance of antagonism as an essential part of human
experience. Finally, we must view memory as both a
pedagogical tool and a subject of the material we read.

My first notion is not new to any teacher: students must
be discoverers. But the meaning of a student as a discoverer
becomes far more powerful if we accept the notion that the
meanings of texts are imbedded in some obscurity, and that the
very nature of the text, its polyvalence and multiple layers
of meaning, actually obligate the reader to be discoverer. It
is one thing to be encouraged to discover a meaning which is
already known by the teacher; it is quite another thing to be
a discoverer of meanings which are hidden from anyone. The
act of reading must be presented as an unfolding of elements,
both clear and obscure, combined with memory of texts and
historical events. But setting out on such a journey without
any instructions can be intimidating--and it is not entirely

honest, since (once again) there are certain meanings which are more or less acknowledged by tradition. Perhaps the teacher can furnish his "discoverers" with a map which is not too detailed, that does not pre-empt their own interpretations.[22] Here, too, the students experience precisely the same tension that is experienced by the teacher: a moderate mixture of normative meanings with the surprise of discovery. A corollary of the division between discovery of meaning and the embracing of a heuristic meaning for the start of the journey is the constant play between the two. Students may develop this very tension as the subject of term papers and examinmations. Where appropriate, a specific topic of the text might actually be the tension between private and public meaning, between manifest and obscure layers of a text, and between its meaning and its significance. Obviously some materials lend themselves more conveniently to this suggestion than others; even meta-meanings cannot exist in equal measure in all texts.

If a reading community is indeed created during the reading of text, then the texts inevitably "contain" aspects of community building, at least on the level of significance or latent meanings. But a meta-topic can be highlighted by calling explicit attention to community as a constant of Jewish life and by selecting materials which reflect this element more explicitly. In addition, the traditional model of small study groups (havruta) can sensitize one to this element. Yet the discoverer must be straining against community, and the individual's acquisition of power through the act of reading and making meanings sets up a conflict which is at the very core of Jewish tradition. Sometimes this conflict appears in the biographical theme which is present-- as subject--within the narrative being read; at other times, it is present only as an implied theme of the entire tradition. Memory--both accurate and faulty--is always at work.

The distance between conflict and antagonism is not very great. When the authority is invested in the teacher, one need not be party to Freudian metaphysics to agree that the teacher must become the object of some struggle when issues of tradition are present. The teacher's task is to assert authority and even to stimulate struggle with it without sabotaging the student's attachment of significance and urge to become discoverer and future authority.

We encourage adherence to authority, on the one hand, and a sense of power to make meaning, on the other. This is far more complicated than teaching a student to wait until he knows enough to be the authority. That day never comes. Clarity about the meanings of texts is as essential as it is dangerous, and teaching is a precarious business. Nowhere is the danger of teaching more evident than in the teaching of texts where so many elements constitute the creation of meaning. Nowhere is it clearer that closure both tantalizes and offends the good teacher, and nowhere is the sense of heuristic approaches more vital for the adherence to authority and the surprise of discovery. Both poles must be served in order to enhance the spirit, and to legitimize the romance with classic texts.

STRUCTURE AND MEANING IN THE WHITE HOTEL

Peggy Ward Corn
The Ohio State University

D. M. Thomas's The White Hotel consists of a sequence of
five distinct narratives: Lisa Erdman's adventures at the
White Hotel as recounted first in the poem and then the
journal, Freud's account of Lisa's psychoanalysis, Lisa's
subsequent life and death, and finally a strange vision of life
after death in a place resembling Palestine. Similarly
constructed works, such as The Golden Notebook and Pale Fire,
belong to a literary category I call Russian doll fictions.[1]
Such works consist of two or more substantial and distinct
narratives; the outermost story contains another story (which
may itself contain a third story, etc.), just as a Russian doll
contains ever smaller dolls within dolls. In a Russian doll
fiction, we understand each story in terms of the other(s), and
the meaning of the work emerges from the interplay of the
narratives. The Russian doll structure of The White Hotel
reveals different components of Lisa Erdman's identity—a
daughter, a wife, a mother, a Jew. We come to know her
intimately enough to be moved by her death at Babi Yar. By
rendering Lisa's life in all its rich emotional complexity,
Thomas makes it possible for us to mourn for someone whose
death would otherwise be a mere statistic. If we can be moved
by Lisa's death, then there is hope that we can begin to
overcome our numbness in the face of large numbers of dead—
like the 250,000 at Babi Yar, or the millions in the
Holocaust—and comprehend the enormity of such a loss in
personal terms.

The novel begins with the innermost of its Russian dolls,
Lisa's poem, and moves outward to a journal that expands on the
poem and provides a larger context for it. Freud's case
history, in turn, explains the first two texts and gives us
more information about their author. This pattern is repeated
in the remaining sections. In this Russian doll fiction, each
succeeding section not only contains the one before but
subsumes it by clarifying and expanding upon it. At the same
time, no one of the novel's narratives is discredited by what
follows. No perspective on Lisa's personality is to be
abandoned just because it is incomplete or inadequate by
itself; rather each must be integrated with all the others, and
each enriches our understanding of Lisa's experience. The
White Hotel attempts to honor the millions of people who died
in the Holocaust by focusing on one of them, showing us just

how much the world lost when this woman, whom one reviewer
calls "a little too ordinary,"[2] died at Babi Yar. The
Russian doll structure invites us to read, interpret, revise
our conclusions, reconsider our revisions, and through that
process come to appreciate the importance of a human life.

Thomas's epistolary prologue is a frame, not an integral
part of the Russian doll pattern which begins with "Don
Giovanni." The frame in this novel performs the same function
as the frame in The Turn of the Screw: the letter from Freud
to Ferenczi and the Freud-Sachs-Kuhn correspondence introduce
the poem and its author, just as the frame in James's story
provides background information on the governess before we read
her manuscript. As in The Turn of the Screw, the characters
who populate Thomas's prologue, with the exception of Freud,
do not reappear in the story itself. At the same time,
however, the letter from Ferenczi to Gisela, which does not
mention Lisa or her writing, introduces motifs that will
reappear in the narratives that follow. The image of the mass
grave first appears in Ferenczi's account of Jung's
conversation about "some 'peat-bog corpses' that apparently
have been found in northern Germany"[3] mummified in a marsh.
Ferenczi's adulterous affair wih Gisela will be echoed in
Lisa's mother's affair, and Lisa's own psychoanalysis is
presaged in Ferenczi's message to Gisela's daughter Elma, who
has also been a patient of Freud's. The frame also serves to
humanize Freud. Ferenczi reports on Freud's rather childish
behavior toward Jung, and on Freud's embarrassment when Jung
interprets a dream in a way that Freud thinks of as challenging
his authority. Thomas will show us that Freud is fallible, and
that he tends to ignore historical forces that inform Lisa's
visions. Even so, the frame fades as we encounter Lisa's poem
and attempt to interpret it. The frame is not subsumed in this
process; it remains outside the novel.

Awkwardly written, powerfully erotic, and very puzzling,
the poem has the quality of a dream or hallucination. What are
we to make of it? "The Gastein Journal" clears up some of our
confusion when it fleshes out the poem's characters and details
events preceding Lisa's stay at the hotel. The journal
provides something like a paraphrase of the poem, but not a
satisfying interpretation. The surreal quality of the poem
carries over into the prose version: the "breast flying
through the yew trees" (p. 64), the heroine's generosity in
providing breast milk with dinner, and the ubiquitous black cat
are some of the details that remain mysterious.

Freud's case history of Lisa as "Frau Ann G." expands our
perspective by supplying facts about the author of the first
two parts and the circumstances in which she composed them.
The "analysis" of psychoanalysis is here largely a matter of
literary interpretation. Freud takes her poem and journal as
keys to the meaning of her pains. When he reads the two, he
begins "to glimpse the meaning behind the garish mask" (p.
133). Her literary work is therefore crucial to his analysis,
as Freud himself acknowledges: "it might teach us everything,
if we were only in a position to make everyting out" (p. 134).
Lisa's unacknowledged homosexual desires, her mother's affair
with her uncle, and her mother's death in a hotel fire, all
surface in analysis, prompted by the imagery of the poem and
journal. By having read Lisa along with Freud, we have come to
know her better and to wish her well. Finally Freud ends their
sessions:

> I told her she was cured of everything but life, so to
> speak. This acceptance of the unalterable past owed much
> to the serenity of Gastein and the subsequent writing of
> her "journal": an interesting example of the unconscious
> preparing the psyche for the eventual release of repressed
> ideas into consciousness (p. 165).

Freud seems to have made sense of her literary productions.
Of course, Lisa's poem and journal are not literary in the
sense that they are carefully constructed and consciously
controlled by their author. Thomas leads us to focus not on
Lisa's skill as a writer but on Freud's skill as a reader.
Freud works out the meaning of the poem and journal according
to consistent principles of interpretation. He seeks out
patterns, coherent themes, unifying ideas; he explains the
symbolism and accounts for the imagery of her work. The
symbolism of Lisa's unconscious--as Freud says, "the repressed
idea creates its own apt symbol" (p. 115)--has been read and
interpreted by the original Freudian critic with great skill.
Lisa is reluctant to accept his discovery of her latent
homosexuality, but that is not an easy fact for many people to
accept, considering the stigma that attaches to homosexuality
even now. Freud's interpretation of the two texts which make
up D. M. Thomas's inner story provides a second context, a
rational one, that explains and thereby subsumes the journal
which has itself provided a context for the poem. Freud
appears to have written the last word on those texts of Lisa's;
we would expect anything that follows to be a postscript,
depicting Lisa's return to normal life. Thomas has revealed

Lisa's inner life to us; now we know her very well, it would seem, but as it turns out there is still a great deal to learn.

Freud's case history ends slightly past the halfway point in the book. The next section reveals that "Anna G." is Lisa Erdman, and it recounts the events of her middle years. Her psychoanalysis is seen in this section not as the most important fact of her life but as merely one phase of it, a phase during which she has learned much about herself, but one which she has moved beyond. Freud's interpretation is subsumed by Lisa Erdman's biography. There appears to be much more to discover about Lisa as the novel continues.

Freud's interpretation of Lisa's writing, which has led to his diagnosis and treatment of what he believes are hysterical symptoms, does not account for all his data on her. Furthermore, it discounts an alternative explanation without seriously considering it. Of course, as every critic knows, texts often have loose ends that cannot be tied up as neatly as one would like. Still, an interpretation need not be exhaustive to be valid and therefore of use to other readers. Freud addresses what is a fact of life for all interpreters: "No analysis is ever complete; the hysterias have more roots than a tree" (p. 164). One detail Freud cannot account for is the specificity of Lisa's pains, mysteriously confined to her left breast and ovary. Unlike Lisa, "The hysteric will tend to describe his pain indefinitely, and will tend to respond to stimulation of the painful part rather with an expression of pleasure than pain" (p. 104). He guesses later that "the left-sidedness arose from a memory that was never brought to the surface" (p. 164), but he can offer no satisfactory explanation for these symptoms. Freud also mentions her short-lived mirror phobia--another loose end.

Lisa Erdman demonstrates to Freud her gift of "second sight," both during analysis and later in her letters, but Freud never considers the possible link between this gift and the meaning of her writings and dreams. To Lisa, her dream about a father who receives a telegram announcing his daughter's death is a prophecy of the death of Freud's daughter. In a letter Lisa tells Freud that, being "cursed with what is called second sight," she "was half convinced that the man who received the telegram was you" (p. 129). Freud, however, interprets it as a dream about news of her own death reaching her father. Later, Freud admits to a belief in telepathy, but he never takes seriously her ability to predict

his future or her own. He explains away the possibility that
she really foresaw his daughter's death in her dream: "It
seems plausible that the patient's sensitive mind discerned in
me anxieties, much below the level of consciousness, over [my]
daughter" (p. 129). In short, telepathy yes, prophecy no.

Freud therefore refuses to consider the poem and journal as
prophetic visions. Anna's fear of motherhood is based on her
belief that something terrible will happen if she has
children. But Freud takes her fear as a symptom, analyzing her
texts as well as her memories and dreams in order to discover
the underlying cause not in the future but in her past.

Just as "Frau Anna G." subsumes Lisa's texts, the fourth
secton, "The Health Resort," the story of Lisa's middle age,
ending with her move to Russia and marriage to Victor
Berenstein, provides a new perspective that comprehends Lisa's
life and work and Freud's interpretation of both. Freud has
changed her name in his case history to protect her privacy,
but the name change has other significance in the larger scheme
of Thomas's novel, the sum of all these parts, in which we see
Freud as a character as well as a reader and writer. The
revelation of her real name in "The Health Resort" points up
the fact that in Freud's case history we get a version of Lisa
Erdman, a Lisa seen from Freud's psychoanalytical perspective.
Freud's Lisa is Anna G., but there is more to Lisa than Freud
has reported in his account. In "The Health Resort" we see
Lisa from another point of view, one not influenced by Freud.
Some readers have remarked that the difference between the Lisa
of "The Health Resort" and the Lisa of "Frau Anna G." is so
great that it produces an inconsistent character. Granted, a
difference exists, but it is not a radical one. Thomas uses it
to emphasize that Freud's case history is an interpretation of
Lisa, a reading, not Lisa herself. As a professional
interpreter of texts, Freud is a writer as well as a reader.
And in creating his own text in response to hers, Freud is
shaping our responses to Lisa's writing. His selection of
detail, his choice of one explanation over another, and above
all his commitment to the principles of psychoanalysis make
Lisa to some degree a literary creation of his. Freud never
claims to be writing biography; his purpose is to show how he
solved a problem and healed a sick woman. Anything irrelevant
to that purpose he omits from his essay. By showing us Lisa
from another perspective, "The Health Resort" helps us to see
that; in this section we read her differently than we did in
Freud's case history. Here Thomas insists on Lisa's

complexity--and by extension the complexity of the
personalities of all the "white hotels" moving toward their
deaths at Babi Yar--by showing us that even Sigmund Freud
cannot understand her completely.

If we are presented with Lisa according to Freud in "Frau
Anna G.," through whose eyes do we see Lisa's life in "The
Health Resort"? Probably they are Lisa's own. The story is
told from a third-person point of view of the most limited
kind; it is an account of Lisa's travels, thoughts, and
feelings as she might write them in a diary. The style is very
simple, even naive. We get no sense of an author's or
narrator's presence detached from Lisa's consciousness,
commenting on her from the outside, as it were. Consider, for
example, a sentence like "her two Russian companions vied with
each other in expressing enthusiasm for their city" (p. 179),
or "understandably the girl had been reserved and a little
resentful; but she was passionately fond of msuic, and found
the afternoons in Lisa's suite . . . so interesting and
instructive that she had shed her unfriendliness" (p. 195).
These flat, lifeless, unsophisticated sentences render Lisa's
thoughts artlessly, as she herself would think them.

Simply put, Lisa's idea of herself is different from
Freud's. Of course, Lisa has changed as a result of her
experience with Freud. In "The Health Resort" we have a Lisa
restored to normal functioning, an ordinary middle-aged woman.
Freud's parting assessment that she has been "cured of
everything but life" seems an apt summary of Lisa's situation.
The analysis has left her feeling better, and with marriage and
a stepson to assuage her loneliness, we have reason to hope
that she will live a happy life.

"The Health Resort" is more than a clumsy postscript to
Freud's carefully crafted case history. The task of reading
and interpretation here passes to Thomas's readers. Freud's
reading begins to be subsumed in ours, and our involvement in
the search for the meaning of Lisa's texts and her life
intensifies. Apart from the three letters from him, one of
which is only summarized, Freud is no longer an actor in this
account of Lisa's life as it progresses--he does not "read" her
anymore. But as readers of Thomas's book, we continue to
formulate hypotheses about the significance of the events of
Lisa's life after analysis. Now it is we who are gathering
data and analyzing it, trying to diagnose her continuing pains
and find a coherent pattern tht makes sense of her life, much
as Freud did in the preceding section. In the course of our

reading of "The Health Resort," the material in Freud's case history and his letters become sources of data for us, part of the text we are reading, his text subsumed by the larger context of the novel as it continues. We then evaluate Freud's interpretation in the light of what we know that he does not. We become revisionists, or, at the very last, metacritics.

In "The Health Resort," new information about Lisa's life comes to light that bears on our reading of the two original texts that Freud analyzed. The section begins with a journey by train to a new life that in some particulars resembles the journey by train to the White Hotel that takes place in "The Gastein Journal." In both narratives Lisa speaks with a young man who is smoking. She is surprised that the train makes a stop "at a tiny Tyrolean village" (p. 172) that is like the "small, quiet station in the middle of the great plain" (p. 38) in her journal. At the station in "The Health Resort" she is also surprised by the number of people who get on the train, just as she had been surprised in "The Gastein Journal" by how many got off the train. Finally, in both cases she thinks of pregnancy: in the journal, she tells the young man that she does not want to become pregnant; in the later section, she notices that all the people who board the train are wearing so much clothing they appear pregnant.

The parallels here--the first of many between this section and the earlier journal--establish the journey by train as a motif that links Lisa's "art" to her life. We begin to see that our interpretation of the novel must account for such links. The novel contains Freud at this point by making him another of its characters; the train motif exists as part of a literary creation controlled and shaped not by Sigmund Freud but by the creator of this fictionalized Freud. There are other patterns of which we become aware in this section. Lisa shares previously withheld information on the incident in her youth which involved, according to her original account as Freud reports it, being frightened by some young sailors who seemed to resent her social status. Now we learn that the experience was actually much worse: some sailors who worked for her father "reviled me for being Jewish" (p. 220). To make their attitude perfectly clear to her, the sailors "spat on me, threatened to burn my breasts with their cigarettes, used vile language [and] forced me to commit acts of oral sex with them," with the result that "from that time I haven't found it easy to admit to my Jewish blood" (p. 221). Freud chooses not to change his manuscript, even though this omission distorts it,

since unlike her he does not attribute her asthma to
self-disgust prompted by the sexual assault. Freud is himself
a Jew, but he consistently ignores her Jewishness in his
analysis. To her letter about the incident Freud replies that
"a postscript in which your later reservations are presented
and discussed" (Op. 230) could be appended to his text, but he
does not follow through. To him her Jewish background is
relatively unimportant to his understanding of her present
pains. But as we come to understand in the sickening scene at
Babi Yar in the next section of the novel, Lisa's identity as a
Jew is the key to interpreting the poem and journal. As George
Levine remarks, Freud's analysis "is clever, if not brilliant,
but its function in the narrative is precisely not to be
adequate."[4]

Another revelation in that same letter also concerns Lisa's
Jewish identity. Freud ignores this information, but Thomas's
readers do not. Lisa has mentioned to Freud that her husband's
family did not like Jews, but their anti-Semitism was worse
than she led him to believe during her analysis. She reveals
in the letter to Freud that she had to lie to her husband about
her Jewish background, which "upset me dreadfully"; more
importantly, it has affected her sexual relations with him and
her reaction to the memory of the affair between her mother and
uncle, two elements of her history that are crucial to Freud's
interpretation. If she is not her father's child, a
possibility raised by the summer-house incident, she is the
offspring of two Gentiles. In that case, "I wasn't Jewish and
I could live with my husband, and get pregnant, with a clear
conscience!" (p. 224). Thus Lisa leads us to an alternative
explanation of her fear of childbirth which, though it does
relate to her mother, has nothing to do with homosexuality. In
the light of this link between her Jewishness and sex, she
re-interprets her experience herself, declaring to Freud that
he "made me become fascinated with my mother's sin, and I am
forever grateful to you for giving me the opportunity to delve
into it," but she rejects it as the key to the pains in her
breast and ovary in the way he has interpreted them. Her
mother's sin "made me unhappy, but not ill" (p. 226), she tells
Freud.

Lisa's pains have not stopped with the end of her
analysis: they recur with greatest intensity at the prospect
of marrying Victor and becoming a stepmother. She hallucinates
and the pains return in full force. Her new husband and
stepchild are Jewish, and we are told that "The political news

everywhere was terrible, and it looked as if worse was to come" (p. 241). When in the novel's penultimate section, "The Sleeping Carriage," poem and journal reveal themselves as symbolic prophecies, we understand that in her twenties Lisa was suffering pains from wounds that had yet to be inflicted. We realize why her Jewish heritage is so important in relation to her pains and fears, and why she was right to avoid motherhood. The imagery of mass death by falling (into the mass grave) and by burial in a landslide (under the bodies of other victims at Babi Yar), the black cat (her friend's pet), all of which appear in the innermost texts, eluded satisfactory analysis by Freud because he read her writing as a manifestation of unconscious fears and desires rather than prophecy. In a sense, the misreading results from a confusion of genre--a dream story must be analyzed by different means than a symbolic prophecy. The misreading also results from Freud's perspective as an analyst of the individual psyche, not an interpreter of world political trends. His Jewishness seems unimportant to him as he analyzes Lisa, just as her Jewishness seemed not to matter to her during the analysis. But it does matter, to both of them. Thomas tells us in a footnote that one of Freud's projects was "abandoned altogether" (p. 151) when the Nazis came to power, and that they burnt his works in Berlin in 1933. He is among the dead in Thomas's version of Palestine at the novel's end, another reminder that even though Freud did not die at the Nazis' hands, they harassed him because he was a Jew. He may choose to define Lisa's identity and his own in terms of personal relationships alone, but he cannot deny the fierce anti-Semitism that engulfs the doctor as well as the patient.

At the end of "The Sleeping Carriage," told from a historical point of view that nonetheless focuses on Lisa's last moments, we find ourselves at a point similar to the one we occupied at the end of Freud's case study: now we understand Lisa's texts. Now we see that Thomas has used the train motif to lead up to the final journey Lisa never takes; now we know why he emphasizes Lisa's Jewish identity even when Freud ignores it, and how sex and death come together horribly at the end of a bayonet. This "reading" of Lisa's texts has the authority of fact, the only real test of a prophecy. This time we can be sure, it would seem, that we know the real meaning of Lisa's stay at the White Hotel.

Yet the question of a final reading of the innermost story told in Lisa's texts is not to be settled by merely replacing

Freud's interpretation with "The Sleeping Carrige." The
pattern in which one section provides a new context that
clarifies and subsumes the preceding context complements the
other pattern in this novel which binds the Russian dolls into
a single novel. Each section uses the same motifs, so that we
are reminded by a theme or incident in, say, "The Health
Resort," of something similar in "The Gastein Journal." These
motifs are not always part of the ongoing work of interpreting
Lisa's illness, do not necessarily explain the previous
imagery, but establish a metaphor for the multi-faceted nature
of the human psyche.

Besides the motif of the train journey, another recurrent
pattern is relations between parents, including surrogate
parents, and their children: Lisa and her Russian friend, Lisa
and her aunt, Lisa and Madame Cottin, Lisa and her understudy,
Freud and his daughter, Lisa and Kolya, and finally Dina
Pronicheva and Motya. Some of these relationships, like some
of the train trips, occur in Lisa's texts, but others happen in
her life, thus running through the novel as a whole. These
motifs, as the reader compares them, unify the sections into a
single novel: they must be considered simultaneously, not just
one after the other. In other words, of the several
perspectives from which we view Lisa--her unconscious, her
analyst, herself, her killers--no one of them invalidates any
of the others: they all contain part of the truth about Lisa.
Each succeeding section provides a new context for what has
gone before, enlarging our sense of the possibilities in
interpreting Lisa's texts. We try to make sense of each
section in the series of contexts the novel provides, finally
interpreting Lisa's life in terms of the manner of her death
and reconciliation with her mother in that odd setting at the
novel's end. At the same time we are interpreting Thomas's
novel: what is its vision of the human soul, of
twentieth-century history, of love and death? We become aware
of Thomas as the ultimate author who creates all these texts
and the connections between them.

At the end of "The Sleeping Carrriage" the most important
feature of Lisa's identity is her Jewishness. Her place in the
history of Europe seems to give us the meaning of her poem and
to define the significance of Thomas's novel in political
terms. But according to the second pattern described above,
which dictates that all the narratives must be taken into
account in deciding on the significance of Lisa's life and
Thomas's novel, there is no one final way of looking at Lisa

that is more credible than any other. This is confirmed in the final section, a sort of afterlife in Palestine, where Lisa reconciles with her mother, the one person whom Freud has helped her to understand, the key figure in his analysis. In this final section Lisa's identity as a Jew in Palestine is co-equal with her identity as her mother's daughter, the crucial relationship in Freud's analysis. The White Hotel, as he interprets it, is Lisa's personal symbol of her mother's womb.

But unlike the other sections, it is difficult to identify a narrator for this final section. Having traced the use of fantasy through the novel, George Levine describes the final section as "another, final, fantasy, but this time it is the novel's, not Elisabeth's alone"; this one is "steeped in reality" because in it "historical suffering remains."[5] But what does it mean to say that the final secton is "the novel's"? Using narrators with a limited point of view has enabled Thomas to make the point that Lisa's soul, or anyone's, presumably, cannot be sufficiently comprehended by any one interpreter. In the last section, however, the narrator seems not to be bound by such restrictions, and that difference may signify that this final section is meant to be the last word, the definitive explanation of Lisa's texts and her life. The problem with this authoritative vision, if it is that, is that Thomas's readers may balk at believing in an afterlife at all. We may be distracted from Thomas's concerns in the novel by wondering whether he means us to believe in an afterlife, especially since the other settings in the book do not strain credulity.[6] Whatever our difficulties with point of view in this last section, Thomas's scheme of subsumption and his employment of a variety of equally valid perspectives culminate in "The Camp." As Carole Kessler has remarked, the "great consoling vision" of "The Camp" shows us that "love has the power to vanquish death." Kessler sees in the tenderness between mothers and children, especially Kolya and Lisa, and Lisa and her mother, "the antidote to pain," not only in Thomas's Palestine but in our world as well.[7] Lisa's killers are not to be allowed the final word on the value of her life.

Taken together, Thomas's multiple perspectives provide an answer to the question of Lisa's identity. Lisa, Thomas tells us, is but one of "A quarter of a million white hotels in Babi Yar" (p. 295). We read her now as a woman formed by a variety of influences, both personal and political. She cannot be accurately understood if any of the perspectives is excluded.

Therefore, her texts must be read as keys to her psyche and as prophecies of the destiny of European Jews. Freud's psychoanalytical interpretation does not take into account her background as a Jew, but the section in which her texts are fulfilled as historical prophecies does not highlight those aspects of Lisa's individual history that loom so large for Freud. Freud's interpretation of Lisa's imagined stay at the White Hotel is subsumed by succeeding narratives not because it is wrong but because it is incomplete. In that last section the location of a place for the dead in Palestine and the presence of Vaska the cat keep before us the fact that Lisa Erdman is dead because she has become Kolya's mother, and because both are Jewish. At the same time, the meeting with her mother reminds us of Freud's role in helping Lisa to understand her mother's importance in her life. In "The Camp," we see how the texts can be understood as significant in political/historical and psychoanalytical terms; both interpretations are right. This last section pulls the book together and insists on the value of the lives of all the white hotels who perished in the holocaust. The Nazis kill their victims, but Thomas denies them a victory over the human soul. Thus the dignity of the human soul, the triumph of love over death that is Thomas's theme in The White Hotel.

THE WINNOWING OF AMERICAN ORTHODOXY

Jeffrey S. Gurock
Yeshiva University

He is the type of Jew seen less and less in today's metropolitan area Orthodox congregations. He is the infrequent Sabbath worshipper who drives to services on holy days but stealthily parks his car around the corner from shul so as not to embarrass himself nor offend his more observant neighbors. His kitchen at home is kosher insofar as biblically forbidden foods are never or rarely served (someone should study the phenomenon of the "chazer pot" in otherwise kosher kitchens), and meat and milk meals and dishes are kept separate. However, he is not overly concerned with the religious reliability of his butcher. The words "Baser Kahser" on the window, sawdust on the floor, and some sort of rabbinic certificate on the wall are proof enough that meats sold within these Jewish precincts were prepared with punctilious regard for ancient and rabbinic ordinances. Moreover, for him, glatt kosher meats are more an economic hardship than a religious desideratum. His commitment to kashruth at home does not extend to cheeses, breads and milks. Indeed, he is probably unaware of halakic considerations in the production of these foods. Outside his home, kashruth observance may be limited to the avoidance of pork and shell-fish dishes and possibly, all non-kosher prepared meats. This "fish-out" eater is, or course, totally at home in his neighborhood kosher delicatessen or restaurant regardless of whether that Jewish settlement is open on the Sabbath or employs a full-time mashgiach (kashruth overseer).

This Jew and his wife do not follow traditional Jewish family purity laws, though his wife may have gone to the mikveh once prior to their marriage. They know of no religious prohibitions limiting the mixing of the sexes socially. They like social dancing both within and without the synagogue, and they may be dismayed that once very popular events like the "synagogue social" no longer appear on Orthodox congregational calendars.

Now in their sixties and seventies, this type of Jew a generation or so ago was the rule, not the exception, in Orthodox congregations. Indeed, throughout the inter-war

period, these American-born children of immigrants were
Orthodoxy's rank and file. They kept the Orthodox synagogue
alive and in the battle against the more liberal denominations
between the end of the era of immigrant Orthodoxy (circa
1880-1920) and the rise of the present generation of resurgent
modern and refugee Orthodoxy. Indeed, these Jews, who defined
their Orthodoxy more as an institutional identification than
as an all encompassing system of beliefs and rituals, may well
have made their denomination the largest among affiliating
Jews until at least 1945. And yet, American Jewish religious
historiography has rarely even noted their existence, let
alone their significance. To be sure, twenty years ago
sociologist Charles Liebman included them in his
undifferentiated category of America's "non-observant
Orthodox." But the processes which kept them loyal to
Orthodox organizational life and the changes both within and
outside their movement that ultimately led to their winnowing
away have not been addressed directly.[1]

Received historical truth has it that the 1920's witnessed
an abrupt change in the fortunes of both Orthodoxy and
Conservatism in America. Prior to that time, it has been
argued, Orthodoxy transplanted from Europe retained a tenuous
hold upon the masses of religiously-identifying immigrant
Jews. It was an Orthodoxy--to be sure--stripped of its
traditional communal coercive powers and unable to keep the
disaffected in line. Still, it served a major socio-religious
purpose for the many new Americans who sought stability and
the comforting reminders of home and shtetl while experiencing
the anomie of the new country's environment. Literally
thousands of small landsmanshaft synagogues gave immigrant
Orthodoxy its most enduring institutional expression. It was
there that Jews from every East European locale were able to
pray and socialize with their own kind even as they preserved
the customs of Zhitomir, Bialystock and Vilna. Significantly,
the Orthodox immigrant's commitment to the faith of the
fathers often did not extend beyod the precincts of the
shtiebl and their culinary practices. Simply put, immigrant
Jews went to shul Friday night to be among friends and to pray
to God and ate only kosher foods because they knew of no other
cuisine, but they went to work on Saturday morning to advance
themselves in America. However, as memories of Europe began
to recede, social attachments to the landsmanshaft system
inevitably loosened. Still, when they went to shul they
expected services to be authentically Orthodox in the European
style.[2]

This form of religiously inconsistent behavior based on nostalgia and the communal elements in synagogue life was incomprehensible to the immigrants' children who were not only Americans but were also imbued early on with the drive for economic mobility and social acceptance. They steadily drifted away from Orthodoxy, their European-based religious identity powerless to stem the tide of assimilation. The ludicrous attempts by leaders of ghetto-based synagogues to attract the "lost generation" back to Judaism through the appointment of charismatic chief rabbis, who stammered Yiddish-language messages to English-speaking listeners, failed utterly. Clearly unpopular with young people by the outbreak of World War I, immigrant Orthodoxy was in danger of losing even its most consistent immigrant generation supporters. Creeping acculturation, if not the actual demise of long time backers, threatened the persistence of that expressison of Judaism.[3]

Orthodoxy's credibility crisis, the historical tradition continues, reached acute proportions when Jews exited from the immigrant ghettos beginning in the early 1920's. As long as Jews had lived downtown, disaffection and assimilation were limited by the homogeneous population of the ghetto environment. Although a Delancey Street Jew in 1900 could announce publicly that he officially renounced his Jewish identity, with whom, on his Jewish block, would he than assimilate? Twenty years later, however, the disaffected Jew could make his boast stick, because Jewish demography had changed. The decade immediately preceding the Great Depression witnessed American history's greatest building boom. In each of this country's great cities, new outer-borough or suburban neighborhoods were built to relieve the tremendous overcrowding wrought by the mass influx of poor whites and blacks into the inner cities during wartime. Middle-class groups of all ethnic and religious stripes flocked to these new residential areas. Immigrant Jews and their children--those possessed of the economic wherewithal to make the move--joined the intra-city migration, settling for the first time in their American experience in mixed neighborhoods. There they clearly had the choice of either continued identification with their faith and people or of complete assimilation into general society. Moreover, during that national era which emphasized conformity of all peoples to American ways, significant external pressure was placed upon the Jew to look and behave like all others. It was there and then, we have been told, that Orthodoxy, European in form and demeanor, unresponsive both to the American environment and to its peoples' changed economic and demographic profile, lost its residual currency with the Jewish masses.[4]

Fortunately for the survival of Judaism, the received truth has taught us, Conservatism was on the scene. (It had been awaiting its chances to serve since 1900, but until that time, most immigrants were not Americanized enough to want it, and their children were not old enough to need it.) Conservatism offered an increasingly large number of Americanizing Jews and their now mature children an alternative to an outdated, irreconcilable Jewish identity and assimilation. Presenting its potential communicants with a compelling, sociologically sophisticated mixture of liturgical traditionalism and ideological liberalism tailored to the new neighborhood life, it emerged during the inter-war period as American Jewry's numerically-predominant denomination--or so we have been told.

Conservative synagogues respected and accomodated the American Jews' desire to pray seated next to their wives as good Americn family men, even as congregants wished to participate in a service which conserved many of the time-honored melodic and liturgical elements of the siddur. Seminary-trained rabbis accorded tacit acceptance-- Conservative legal approval came later on--to family decisions to drive to services on Sabbaths and holidays because the sanctuary was miles away from their homes. Synagogues changed the times of Friday and holiday night prayers, recognizing that outer-borough commuters employed in inner city trades, professions and emporia could not always easily attend sundown services. And they provided congregants with an array of ancillary services--dances, movies, lectures, athletics--all within their synagogue centers. Furthermore the Conservative Movement cast all these developments in the mold of older Jewish philosophical and practical traditions, facilitating the communicants' continued identification with the faith's useable past while living and praying as American. So conceived and instituted, the Conservative Movement--some 260 United Synagogues of North American congregations strong by 1928--lured those masses of Jews who readily abandoned Orthodoxy away from complete assimilation and back towards Judaism.[5]

Inter-war's Orthodox rank and file would not have agreed with this widely-accepted narrative. For them, abandoning the

piety of immigrant Orthodoxy and the comfort of the
landsmanshaft did not leave them either bereft of a Jewish
identity or in search of a new religious way of life. To
begin with, though they had moved to new, better-built
residential areas towards the outskirts of the city, they
still resided in highly-homogeneous Jewish neighborhoods. As
one most perceptive Jewish urban historian has shown, the
streets of New York's Astoria and the Grand Concourse were no
less Jewish than those of the ghetto's Allen and Delancey.
One could be Jewish and, indeed, marry Jewish by living and
socializing on one's Jewish block. Jews of this period met
their own kind in schools, at the work place, at public and
private social clubs and the like. They did not always need
the synagogues to serve as the rallying central Jewish
institute, though to be sure the Conservative synagogues of
that time offered themselves as such. Like their fathers
before them, once acculturated they saw the synagogue
primarly--if not exlusively--as a place where one came to
pray. And Jews came to pray when they felt the personal need
in times of family crises, in commemoration or in memorial of
significant life cycle events, or during the High Holy Days.
At these times, Orthodox Judaism's rank and file wanted to
pray in the most authentic, legitimate (read "effective")
way. And that meant in an Orthodox synagogue, albeit one
possessed of some modern accoutrements.[6]

For this constituency of Jews, the transfer of their
allegiance to emerging Conservatism--or for that matter to
fledgling Neo-Reform--required that they both needed and were
committed to those liberal expressions of Judaism. But
neither the need nor the commitment was yet strongly in place
within their religious mind-set. The Jews of Flushing, New
York, did not need their synagogues to postpone wintertime
erev shabbos service from early sundown to after dinner
because of the propinquity of their homes to stores and other
work places in the 1920's-1930's. The Manhattan-based
merchant could get home to Queens in time to attend services
scheduled according to Judaism's clock; that is, of course, if
he had a driving commitment to attend services at all after a
hard week in the American workplace.

Moreover, Orthodox Jews did not need to sit next to their
wives during prayer services, though if they had had their
druthers they probably would have preferred to do so. But to
their minds the joys of mixed seating were not substitute for
the serenity they felt in knowing that their prayers in days

of crisis or of judgments were being offered to the Almighty in his most traditional of houses.

Rank and file Orthodox Jews ultimately could not accept Conservative teachings and religious procedures as legitimate, even as their personal behavior ran far afield of what Orthodoxy preached. So disposed, hedging their bets in this world and the world to come, they searched for a type of synagogue that would not embarrass them as Americans--although travel back to the Lower East Side shteibl to observe papa's yahrzeit was not uncommon--but would at the same time keep the lines of communication open to Providence.

Fortunately for them, they found American Orthodox synagogues ready to accomodate their religious needs and social desires. Offering acculturating East European Jews "dignified services" noteworthy for their insistence upon decorum, weekly sermons in the vernacular, and supplementary English-language prayers while retaining the core of traditional tefillah and Orthodoxy's understnading of time and seating configurations, Orthodox synagogues, in fact, had been waiting for them as early as 1900. In 1901, the Jewish Endeavor Society, founded by the early students and first rabbis produced by the pre-Solomon Schecter Jewish Theological Seminary, set up shop on the Lower East Side, in Harlem and in Philadelphia "to recall indifferent Jewry--those disaffected from the landsmanshaft synagogue--back to their ancestral faith." Some 10 years later, the Young Israel movement was inaugurated "to bring about a revival of Judaism among the thousands of young Jews and Jewesses whose Judaism is at present dormant." And in 1917-1918, the Institutional Synagogue and the Jewish Center Synagogue were established in Harlem and New York's West Side, respectively, to serve the acculturated resident one-step removed from the ghetto. Their New York-based institutions inspired comparable synagogue life-styles in cities and communities nationwide.[7]

Significantly, in each of these pre-World War I endeavors, potential communicants were offered more than just the chance to pray as an American. Displaying features later and more widely seen as characteristic of the Conservative synagogue center, these institutions promoted a wide range of ancillary synagogue activities--lectures, dances, movies, athletics. Moreover, no questions were asked about one's personal observance outside of synagogue precincts. Synagogue leaders understood that theirs was the task of "drawing back" towards tradition those disaffected, regardless of their clients' religious commitment at the moment of encounter.[8]

These early activities were, however, only minimally successful. Like their early Conservative counterparts, American Orthodox too found that most immigrants were not Americanized enough to want their services, and their children were still too young to need them. Additionally, so long as these American Orthodox worked where Old-World Orthodoxy still held sway among the faithful, the modernizing encountered frequent, stridently expressed opposition from transplanted Russian rabbanim. Rabbi David Willowsky, the so-called Radbaz, was probably the most famous opponent of sociological change. He once declared that adoption of even the seemingly innocuous English-language sermon "would leave no hope for the continuance of the Jewish religion." But there were others also. As one JES member explained: "Our services were successful but unfortunately a maggid usually appeared on the scene followed by his hosts and naturally, the services had to move to make room for the Yiddish preachers." Inspired by the maggid's public comments, a family's raised eyebrows may have deterred some young people, albeit uncomfortable with their fathers' landsmanshafts, from joining, with a clear conscience, the rabinically castigated new religious societies.[9]

Still, the idea that the Orthodox synagogue must accomodate its constituency, accept all who seek its precincts, and make them comfortable there as Americans and as Jews, regardless of their personal religious observance, were ideas that survived into the 1920's. And between the wars these ideas became articles of faith for out-borough or suburban congregations, led by American-trained rabbis produced by the Rabbi Isaac Elchanan Theological Seminary (RIETS), the rabbinical-training arm of what is today Yeshiva University.

But RIETS did not begin as a seminary for the training of American rabbi. When founded in 1897, it was a transplanted East European Yeshiva providing immigrant students and scholars with an opportunity to continue their religious learning. Only after a decade of pressure from, among others, Americanized Orthodox East European lay leaders was RIETS reorganized as the Rabbinical College of America. Under the leadership of Rabbi Bernard Revel, the school slowly began to produce rabbis knowledgeable in American ways and able to preach in English homiletic messages attractive to fellow second generation Jews--worthy opponents of JTS graduates.[10]

Once in the field--either in Young Israel or Orthodox Union (OU) congregations situated outside of the inner city--these young Orthodox rabbis quickly discovered not only that most potential communicants were moving away from personal, all-encompassing Orthodoxy, as already had been the case in the ghetto, but that the newly popular, traditional denominations accepted them without question. Accordingly, they recognized that if they took a hard line towards members' non-observance--either through pulpit excoriation or through the denial of membership or synagogue honors--and if they ignored demands to push ritual and the synagogue's ancillary activities to the limits of Jewish law, they would find themselves without a congregation and without a pulpit. To help Orthodoxy's rank and file within the synagogue and to prevent them from looking into the more liberal denominations, inter-war American Orthodox rabbis followed the congregations's desires--even if they did not agree with them at the outset--to bestow synagogue membership and honors upon individuals known to be Sabbath violators and even to welcome into congregational lists men who had married out of the faith. And it was patently understood that the rabbi would come down from his study to greet members when they attended mid-week synagogue socials. The rabbi might also dance with the synagogue president's wife at the congregational banquet, if lay politics ordained a waltz with the rabbi. Inter-war, Orthodox Jewry thus found their synagogues a most accepting and accomodating environment. The Orthodox synagogue was there when they needed it. It was organized and maintained along American lines and made no great demands upon their personal religious deportment.[11]

This "half-baked laity, with a confused and distorted view of Judaism whose personal observance of mitzvoth has vanished to a great extent," as one St. Louis-based rabbi defined his community's rank and file, was comfortable enough with the Orthodox synagogue to constitute the single largest element in inter-war Orthodoxy. More than the remnants of immigrant Orthodoxy and these later-to-be-called "modern Orthodox," this, at first, a small contingent of the acculturated who deemed Orthodoxy important--if not central--to their private as well as their public lives, populated the estimated 900 Orthodox Union synagogues in 127 cities in twenty-seven states coast to coast. And to a lesser extent they predominated in the thirty-two New York and East Coast, out of ghetto-based Young Israels, whose members seemingly practiced more consistently what they prayed. Indeed, if one adds to the Orthodox rank and file a third, equally understudied segment of American Jewry--those Jews who joined the so-called "traditional Orthodox synagogue" which proliferated outside of the East Coast and which followed all Orthodox synagogue rituals and traditions, save separate seating--one would probably find that that mixed aggregate (rank and file Orthodox and traditional synagogue members) all recognized as "Orthodox" by the OU might well substantiate the 1937 boast that it represented "the largest Jewish religious group numerically in the United States."[12]

Certainly in New York City, outside of Manhattan, even when one excludes the "traditional synagogues" from the calculations, Orthodox synagogues more than held their own. In the 1920's and 1930's, Queens and Long Island were served by eleven USA congregations and by an estimated nineteen OU synagogues. In the Bronx, eleven Conservative Temples were matched by as many Orthodox synagogues and in Brooklyn's new Flatbush, Bensonhurst and Borough Park neighborhoods, the Brooklyn Jewish Center and sixteen other Conservative congregations competed with fourteen Young Israel affiliates. Significantly, in this and in other cities, both USA and OU Congregations bore the names "Jewish Center," highlighting the similarity of the services offered in both institutions. Nationally, when one adds the traditional Orthodox to the outer-city rank and file Orthodox total, similar statistics emerge.[13]

The winnowing of Orthodoxy's rank and file began after World War II. It was equally a result, on the one hand, of changes in Jewish demography, sociology and religious psychology and, on the other, of the increasingly exclusionary attitudes taken by the Orthodox synagogues towards the marginally observant. To begin with, the post-war Conservative and Neo-Reform approaches to synagogue life, far more than those of the 1920's-1930's, suited well Jewish suburban-sprawl life. Now men and women truly worked far away from their homes, and their homes were many miles from their temples. Thus, whereas the 1920's Jewish merchant working in Manhattan could conceivably have closed his store and made it home to Astoria for Friday evening services, his son or daughter, a 1950's-1960's Wall Street attorney living in Levittown, Long Island definitely could not. And why, for that matter, should they have tried? Unlike their ancestors, they were psychologically comfortable as followers of legitimate middle-class expressions of Judaism which formally countenanced their driving to services and encouraged family participation in all synagogue rituals. Armed with their denomination's imprimatur, post-World War II Conservative and Reform synagogue members felt no guilt regarding their un-Orthodox behavior. Unlike his father--as we portrayed him at the outset--who drove to Orthodox services and parked his car out of sight of others, the Levittowner unabashedly left his car in the Temple's parking lot. Finally, when they arrived--whether they were Conservative or Neo-Reform--they felt very much in touch with Judaism's ancient revered traditions; the prayers sounded like those in the American Orthodox synagogue. God, they were reassured, would harken to their petitions and supplications even if the older formulas were accompanied by an organ or guitar.[14]

But what of their "parents" and, to a lesser extent, those of the younger generation still unconvinced of the legitimacy and efficacy of liberal denominational theory and practice? They followed the Orthodox synagogue as it too moved from outer-borough or outer-city limits to the new suburbia, with the anticipation that shuls would continue to accept and accommodate their deviant religious behavior. And in some localities, particularly in towns and suburbs removed from New York and its environs, their expectations were fulfilled. Where Orthodoxy became a beleaguered minority in the heartland of Conservatism and Neo-Reform, synagogues and rabbis followed the now time-honored tradition of overlooking members' heterodoxy. Not so the synagogues and rabbis of New York and other post-war Eastern Orthodox hubs. There, to an ever increasing degree, the resolute, minimally committed Orthodox as opposed to those desirous of becoming more personally observant, the so-called baalei teshuvah of all ages, were no longer admitted to and/or were made to feel uncomfortable with synagogue life.[15]

In New York and elsewhere, RIETS graduates and others of even more traditional yeshiva training stood strongly against mixed social activities and functionally dismantled other ancillary features. Moreover, they subtly--when not overtly--disenfranchised minimally committed members by establishing as norms for full congregational integration the punctillious adherence to kashruth, Sabbath and family purity laws. These contemporary Orthodox rabbis could take hard-line approaches without risking their position because for the first time in American synagogue history there now existed within their communities a large, growing coterie of mostly younger Jews who shared and desired this strict orientation.[16]

These committed cohorts were more often than not the modern Orthodox triumphalist children of interwar Jewry's small modern Orthodox survivalist contingent. They did not consider themselves a threatened minority seeking out a minyan among their brethren. Better educated than their elders and those in the provinces, these products of post-1945 Jewish day schools were more secure in, or at least were better able to compartmentalize Jewish traditions and American mores, than were their talmud-torah/heder-educated parents, even as the definitions of modern Orthodox behavior moved steadily to the right. And convinced as they were that they and their fellow day-school graduates could insure Orthodoxy's continuity without the assistance of those less committed than themselves, they felt no impulse to worship with those who had drifted from their Jewish norms. They certainly did not have their parents' close personal and social links with and sensitivity towards the less observant. (Remember that a generation or so ago, modern and rank and file Orthodox children sat side by side in large synagogues or communal talmud torahs. Today, day schools are for the modern Orthodox and the children of baalei teshuvah, and Orthodox talmud torahs, at least in New York, are dying.) Moreover, the committed cohort's conceptions of the synagogue--their synagogue agendas--were fundamentally different from those of the older rank and file. For the triumphalists' younger generation, the synagogue was not primarily a ritual, commemorative and memorial domain. Nor was it really a center for the intensification of Jewish identity. Rather it was a home where the already committed could assemble, study and pray--the synagogue's age-old function even in the most modern of architectural settings--helping them increase their familiarity with tradition beyond what they had learned of it in school.[17]

The increasingly confident stance of those educated in day schools was strengthened by the slow movement into their neighborhoods and into their synagogues of another highly committed, newly emerging constituency: refugee Orthodoxy's second generation. These individuals were the now grown children of the immigrants who fled to America from Germany and Eastern Europe during and after Hitler's reign with their devotion to the maintenance of Eastern European Orthodoxy

well-nigh intact. Their parents were the Jews who, during the
classical period of East European migration, had heeded the
words of the Chofetz Chaim: "Whoever hopes for the continuity
of Judaism will not come to America."[18] Arriving in this
country during the late 1940's-early 1950's, these refugees
set about under the guidance of survivor Roshei Yeshiva to
transplant the so-called yeshiva world in the United States.
The remarkable institutions they created were matched only by
their ability to keep so many of their second-generation
children closely bound to their father's faith, an
accomplishment unique in the annals of American Jewish
history.[19]

     And yet the children of Orthodox refugees were not totally
immune to Americanization, at least, not to its economic
aspect. Young graduates of transplanted yeshviot aspired
towards economic mobility. They wanted to be doctors,
accountants, lawyers, computer scientists, and other positions
and profesisons which clearly required secular education, even
if they ultimately felt more comfortable in the yeshiva.
Fortunately for them, they sought professional higher
education during an era when American universities permitted
individuals to graduate from their schools without large-scale
exposure to the assimilatory liberal arts. Schools--public
and private, Ivy League too--even gave transfer credit for
yeshiva education, not only because the business of education
changed, but just as importantly, because of America's quest
during and since the cold-war era to train the best and the
brightest. Americanization, consequently, was no longer a
prerequisite for advancement in American society.
Accordingly, in the 1960's and after, children of refugees
rose from ghetto poverty to affluence in the fashionable
middle- and upper middle-class urban and suburban
neighborhoods without losing their commitment to Orthodoxy,
fundamentalist in content and slightly American aesthetic in
tone. There they linked arms with--and indeed have influenced
significantly--their day-school-trained co-religionists in
creating a contemporary synagogue life committed to the study
of traditional law and its maintenance with modern
conveniences. Indeed, when these Jews talked about
socio-religious ancillary activities, their concerns were with
eruvim (enclosures permitting carrying on the Sabbath day)
which allowed observant parents to wheel baby carriages to
services, thus enabling the Orthodox family to stay together
while praying together--albeit on opposite sides of a
mechitza.[20]

This new era Orthodox synagogue tacitly winnowed out the aging rank and file Orthodox Jew. To be sure, the less observant elderly "member" still perceived the Orthodox sanctuary as God's most--or only--authentic house. But he found that God's--or rather Orthodox Judaism's---requirements had become stricter than ever. Glatt kosher meats, cholev Yisroel cheese, mikvehs and eruv building campaigns were the issues central to the younger, more educated members' lives. The synagogue's agenda projected concerns foreign to him. The older rank and file Jew had been moved from the core of his denomination to the periphery, and he is today destined for extinction. His descendants have already found--or will find--their places in more liberal denominations or among the assimilated. They may, of course, find their ways towards affiliation with the rising numbers of committed Orthodox. But the entry requirements for such initiates are becoming more stringent day by day.

THE AGEING OF REFORM

Daniel Jeremy Silver
The Temple, Cleveland

Reform enjoys all the external trappings of success. In
1954 there were 447 congregations with some 900,000 members
affiliated with the movement. In 1984 there are 770
congregations with a membership of 1,250,000. Over the same
period Reform's national presence, the UAHC, has quadrupled
its budget and more than doubled its staff. More young people
apply to the HUC-JIR for rabbinic and cantorial training than
can be accommodated. There is a vigorous youth and camp
program. In a few cities congregations have given birth to
day schools. The numbers are positive, but some of us who
labor in the vineyard sense that the upward curve is losing
steam and that such growth as there is results more from
inertial energy than increased interest or intense
commitment. I would describe Reform in 1984 as a movement
lacking coherence--a movement in search of itself.

Let me illustrate what I mean by incoherence. In 1975 the
CCAR published a new siddur. The Gates of Prayer was widely
welcomed since it made possible an ampler and more colorful
service than the old Union Prayer Book. Today most Reform
Jews want to be more demonstrably Jewish--at least in the
synagogue--but the Gates' assertive Jewishness masks an
underlying confusion about Judaism. Whatever its stylistic
failings, the language of the Union Prayer Book refracted a
rather consistent and surprisingly traditional theology. God
was a personal God who heard Israel's prayers. The soul lived
on with God. In contrast, the editors of Gates published side
by side liturgies which expressed contradictory theological
positions. In one Sabbath service, which the editors call
"traditional," prayer is addressed to the God of Abraham,
Isaac and Jacob, Sarah, Rebecca, Rachel and Leah, a personal,
if gender-conscious, God. Another service restricts itself to
images drawn from the language of religious naturalism. There
is even one service whch is avowedly humanistic: the Borechu
and the Shema are not translated and the English text makes no
mention of God. "Adonai Sefatai Tiftach," "Lord, open my lips
that my mouth may declare your glory" becomes "may our lips
and our lives be one in serving eternal truths."

To put the best possible face on this theological
smorgasbord, the editors indicate in their introduction that
there are many paths to heaven's gates. This prayer and that
one, this service and that one, may both have the power of
leading us to the living God. Open-mindedness is an
attractive virtue--at least to those whose beliefs are
uncertain--but, historically, one of a siddur's functions has
been to lift up Judaism's central affirmations. From this
perspective Gates reflects not a return to tradition, as
reviewers have claimed, but a novel and radical departure.
Its eclecticism, which few congregants have noticed, suggests
that whatever be the shared commitments that bind most Reform
Jews to their congregations, they are not to be located in the
area of theology. Some years ago I chaired a Commission on
Identity for the CCAR. We wanted to understand our own, so we
interviewed congregants in New York City, Richmond, and
Cleveland about their motives for affiliation. Their most
common response was to praise Reform's open-mindedness: "My
congregation lets me believe whatever I want to."

Piety is not Reform's long suit. Indeed, piety is not a
particular strength of any segment of America Jewry, but this
lack is particularly noteworthy in Reform because Reformers
consciously set out to distinguish and refurbish the spiritual
elements of Judaism which they believed had become lost from
view under the overgrowth of medieval practice. I. M. Wise
defined Reform "as an effort to rescue Judaism from
indifferentism, desertion and ignorance, by inspiring
Israelites with a love of Judaism and by a return to
essentials."

The European disciples of Reform accepted the discipline
of weekly public worship, as did the first generation or two
of their descendants here. My congregation, founded in 1850
by Central European Jews, has kept accurate attendance records
since World War I. From 1917 to 1927 almost all the two
thousand seats of The Temple were filled for the major weekly
service. During each of the four subsequent decades, decades
of membership growth, attendance fell by half. Today, in
synagogues across the land, only a determined and often
elderly minority still treat public worship as a required act
of devotion. We used to speak of revolving-door Jews, in on
Rosh Hashanah, out on Yom Kippur. My Commission found that
one in two members of Reform congregations did not attend
services on both High Holidays. People do come to their
synagogue: when someone they care about is being honored with

an aliyah, for the bar mitzvah of a friend's child, or to say
Kaddish. In the 1980's it is the ties of family rather than
the ties of faith which are central.

Let me add another bit of evidence which illustrates
Reform's present lack of ideological coherence. In 1971 a
CCAR committee was named to prepare a Centennial Platform for
the movement. The first Platform had been adopted in
Pittsburgh in 1885. The second, which was accepted in
Columbus in 1936, signaled, among other things, the end of
Reform's institutional anti-Zionism. The third Platform was
destined to be stillborn. Colleagues met and found that they
could not agree on many essentials, so, because they could not
admit that Reform was a movement without a message, they
decided to prepare a document that would be called a Centenary
Perspective which would list various popular opinions. The
editors worked hard to make a virtue of necessity: "Reform
Judaism," they wrote, "does more than tolerate diversity; it
engenders it." The subsequent Biennial of the UAHC hailed
"diversity within unity" as the "hallmark of Reform." To many
observers the inability of the rabbis to formulate a broad
consensus suggested that Reform's unity, such as it is, is
institutional and fraternal rather than theological or
ideological.

When we asked our interviewees why they had joined a
Reform congregation, we were told: "It's where we were
brought up," "To be with our friends," "The synagogue is
convenient," "I want my kids to meet the kids who go there,"
"This temple seems to fit my needs," "I like their lecture
series and programs," "It has a good school and no one
intrudes on my life." Issues of faith rarely surfaced. For
many it seemed to make no difference if their synagogue was
Reform, Conservative, or Reconstructionist. When we asked
membership committee chairmen what prospective members wanted
to know they told us: cost of membership, Bar Mitzvah
requirements, and cemetery privileges. The only halachic
issue which was sometimes raised focused on whether the rabbi
would perform an intermarriage. We almost concluded that the
only definition we could come to was that Reform Jews are
those who pay dues to Reform congregations.

In the middle of the 19th century, Abraham Geiger wrote
that Reform proposed to renew the Jewish people as a community
of faith. It hasn't quite worked out that way. If I were to
describe today's Reform polity, I would say that it represents
those American Jews who are non-Orthodox, who have no strong

theological hangups, who desire to have their children identify with the Jewish people and, at the same time, be able to mingle easily in the larger community, and for whom some of the traditional life cycle customs still have appeal.

Are there no common beliefs? There are, but, for the most part, these beliefs derive from the political world rather than from the area of spiritual concerns. The president of a congregation where I recently led a seminar on Jewish identity told me that he was sure no one heard our prayers. He wasn't sure if there was anyone out there. Why then did he bother with the many burdens of a congregation? "The worlds needs Jews." Why? "To keep the flame alive." What flame? "The flame of social consciousness. Power corrupts. People are callous. The world needs people with a Yiddische kopf and neshamah."

My experience as a rabbi suggests that two broad areas of conviction energized Reform: commitment to the survival of the Jewish people together with some feeling that this people exhibits special qualities, and the conviction that the Reform synagogue should affirm and confirm a liberal political agenda, including social welfare, civil rights, the separation doctrine. . . .

Most Reform Jews respond to Fackhenheim's eleventh commandment: do not give Hitler a posthumous victory. Yom ha-Shoah and Yom ha-Atzmaut are routinely included in congregational schedules. Twenty years ago the Hebrew Union College decided to send all freshmen rabbinic students to Jerusalem for a year. There is now a Reform Zionist movement, ARZA. Two Reform kibbutzim are in place. Peoplehood is no longer an issue. Classical Reform opposed Jewish nationalism, but today Reform Jews find confirmation in their synagogues for their deepest emotions about the Holocaust and Israel.

While Israel and the Holocaust remain compelling themes for American Jews and the Reform synagogue, the love affair between the Reform synagogue and a progressive political agenda seems to be having more than its share of problems.

Thirty years ago the political liberalism of the majority of American Jews and Reform's doctrine of prophetic mission made beautiful music together. Liberal rabbis extolled Amos, described the human being as God's designated partner in the work of Creation, and encouraged their flock to believe that the well-documented political liberalism of Americn Jews derived from mainstream Judaism. These rabbis did not focus on the vexing question: Why, if this were so, did the polls

show that the more observant a Jewish group the more
conservative its political cast?

Over the last thirty years the resolutions of the UAHC,
Reform's national body, have mirrored the attitudes of
so-called progressive political circles. Reform opposed
nuclear testing, the war in Vietnam, apartheid in South
Africa, war-time conscription; and supported Cesar Chavez, the
Humphrey-Hawkins full employment bill, the ERA, full civil
rights for homosexuals, restitution for American Indians and
Japanese-American internees, mandatory school busing to
achieve desegregation, non-segregated public housing, the Poor
People's Campaign, abortion reform, and a national energy
policy. At its most recent biennial the UAHC demanded that
human rights criteria be applied strictly before military or
economic assistance is granted in Latin America, and that
Washington refrain from destabilizing any government in the
area; reaffirmed its commitment to economic justice for women,
citing particularly the areas of insurance, pension, and
Social Security benefits; attacked cuts in programs serving
the elderly, including food stamps, low-income winterization,
home energy assistance, and Medicare; called on the government
to delay deployment of the Cruise and Pershing II missiles;
and demanded a superforce to deal effectively with hazardous
toxic waste. I suspect a statistician could easily establish
a substantial correlation between the resolutions of the UAHC
and those of the Democratic Party and between those of the
CCAR and those of Americans for Democratic Action.

I have no particular quarrel with this agenda. My point
is analytic, not judgmental. Religions can be defined as
particular clusters of ideas, virtues, institutions, myths,
and ceremonies which declare a particular set of values to be
redemptive. My point is that since at least the end of World
War II that cluster of ideas, virtues, institutions, myths and
ceremonies which Reform's institutions and members have
accepted as redemptive derived primarily from the world of
politics, and that in the 1980's those particular political
ideas are not as compelling as they once were. The post-war
generation of Reform Jews found in Reform confirmation of
certain cherished political beliefs, and the institutions of
Reform often let their responsibility stop there. What was
called prophetic Judaism was often a political statement more
than a statement of concern about Jewish religious life. When
the UAHC established a lobbying center in Washington to

promote its social concerns, this building was at first innocently named Social Action Center. Only after the building was dedicated did the leadership remember what we claim--that our ethical principles derive from the religious tradition, from God rather than social theory--and belatedly renamed it Religious Action Center. Note: even then it was not named "Jewish Action Center."

In the immediate past it was not at all unusual to find some of the leadership treating worship and relgious education not as ends in themselves but as consciousness-raising techniques. One example crossed my desk a few weeks ago: a 20-page brochure from the UAHC showing how Shabbat Ha-Gadol could be used to make people sensitive to environmental issues. We are encouraged to add to the liturgy readings like this:

> In the beginning God created the heavens and the earth. The earth was without form and void, and darkness was upon the face of the land; and the spirit of God was moving over the face of the waters.

> In the beginning of the technological age, man recreated the heavens and the earth, to the earth he gave new form with dynamite and bulldozer, and the void of the heavens he allied with smog.

Other suggestions included having a "resource conservative" (sic) Oneg after the service "where the goodies would be made using recipes which did not require energy." It was also suggested that during the service the rabbi turn off the lights for a few minutes to illustrate our dependence on energy. The theme of this brochure is to provide "a Jewish perspective on the environment," but in fact such a service simply tried to give a Jewish hechsher, certificate of authenticity, to a set of political ideas. If this were not so, such manipulation of the sacred would never be tolerated.

In recent years Jewish needs, and therefore Jewish attitudes, which began in the nineteenth century have changed rather dramatically. The breakdown of the traditional Jewish community, with emigration, urbanization and industrialization, created an uprooted proletariat which was readily attracted to the socialist ideologies popular in Eastern Europe. The political use of anti-semitism by the opponents of social change identified the political Right with the enemy. In America the congruence of the liberal agenda with the aims of an upwardly mobile second generation community solidified the shidduch. In the years after World

War II many newly successful Jews looked about and decided that far-reaching social welfare legislation provided the best possible guarantee against the emergence in America of the kind of social dislocation and economic chaos whch had spawned Naziism. They were also affectd by the fact that progressive political ideas were the accepted gospel in the Village Voice and among certain highly visible groups of the intelligentsia, and many Jews had a desperate need to feel that they were in the intellectual vanguard.

That was yesterday. Today a new set of experiences is reshaping the American Jewish political consciousness. There has been a loss of faith in old-line liberalism, born of many causes. Government over-regulation is one. The stagnation of the economy and the cost of government are others. Jewish financial and social success is a third. The standard measurements of education, occupational status, and income suggest that in the 1980s in time the Jewish community may be America's most successful ethnic or religious group. The successful want to hold on to what they have, though having known more than a few socialist-minded Jewish millionaires, I would weigh political experience as far more important than prosperity as the major cause of liberalism's fall from grace. Jews have learned that our enemies are not all on the Right. Jews have seen dictatorships of the Left in Russia, Poland, Czechoslovakia, Nicaragua, and Cuba make common cause with the PLO. A majority of socialist and Third World countries voted for the infamous U.N. resolution defining Zionism as racism. From Cuba in the 1950's to Nicaragua in the 1980's, countries which underwent socialist revolutions invariably witnessed an exodus of Jews. The passion for absolute equality has been seen to require a degree of state control that bodes ill for Jews. Regimented societies have no room for a non-conforming people.

The old liberal is still there, but five Arab wars, affirmative action legislation, the budget deficits, and Jesse Jackson have led many to abandon Amen-saying and contributed to a growing suspicion that an activist policy of social planning may not have all the answers. Many Reform Jews are reading Commentary and Public Affairs and are asking how the rabbi can approve of affirmative action when it discriminates against their children or how the UAHC can be indifferent to the tax cost of welfare legislation.

Reform could enjoy the luxury of being theologically incoherent as long as its members found in the synagogue the confirmation of the civic virtues and political values they brought to it. But what happens when a sizable number of people in Reform congregations begins to lose faith in the cluster of social values which the synagogue has been proclaiming as redemptive? To thrive, even to survive, religious movements require that their cluster of redemptive ideas remain compelling to the community.

Jews, like everyone else, have been made uneasy by the continuing and unremitting pace of political and social change. The air is full of conflicting advice. People don't know where to turn. They want someone--God--to speak with confidence and certainty. People--Jews--seek roots and direction. We see evidence of this in the new-found popularity of evangelism and religious orthodoxy, in the renaissance of Moral Majority rhetoric, in the back-to-basics movement, in the appeal of the cults and in the compelling simplicities of popular music. In 1954 Bishop John Robinson proclaimed the death of God. Thirty years later the Senate engaged in a bruising fight over a Prayer Amendment. God is no longer an idea which must be discarded by anyone who wishes to be thought an intellectual. Harvey Cox has described the (to some) unexpected renewal of religious passion in his recent book, Religion in the Secular City. America's upper middle-class churches, long the bastion of a non-theological humanistic Christianity, have taken up spiritualism and Christology. This is the age of Jerry Falwell, not Richard Neibuhr.

Though many of us are disturbed by the passions which have been aroused, we cannot doubt the need for balance and the need to hold on to certain personal and familiar virtues which motivate the Ba'alei Teshuvah. Every rabbi has faced the bitter parent whose child went off to college from a spiritually starved home and was picked up by some evangelical movement or cult. Where was the warmth and the sense of community, the living faith, the child claims not to have found?

Surprisingly, the American Jewish community, usually so quick off the mark, has been one of the last to respond to these new needs. Ten years ago when Leonard J. Fein surveyed members of Reform synagogues, he discovered "a powerful, perhaps even desperate, longing for community." His interviews convinced Fein that many rabbis had recognized this need but had not been able to restructure their congregations to respond effectively. Why not? As an explanation Fein posited what he called "the prevalence of opinion as a substitute for belief . . . the existence of belief but the absence of any belief systems." Reform members had few strong convictions, so there were few strong ties to which the rabbis could appeal. Many clearly wanted something--encouragement, a sense of purpose, a sense of the sacred--but Fein found that they were not yet ready to suspend disbelief long enough to allow them to enter wholeheartedly the experience of faith. Many of the Reform Jews I meet remind me of smokers who talk about quitting, but do not yet acknowledge that they must. They would like to believe, to be part of, but they can't bring themselves to put aside their humanistic conditioning, which convinced them that religion is a human invention, to listen to the voice which commands them to reshape their lives. Judaism involves disciplines, but Reform Judaism has neglected discipline.

Because the support of liberalism has become problematic, Reform needs to draw together a broader, more attractive, and more specific definition of religious obligation. There are indications that some in Reform have begun to recognize the problem. For example, the new prayer book describes certain duties as mitzvot. Last November at its Biennial the UAHC adopted a resolution whose preamble recognized "an urgent need for renewed examination of that which religious commitment implies for us and our congregations" and resolved "to engage in a two-year study of this challenge in all its manifestations . . . to generate a suggested programmatical response." But these moves are still taken gingerly. Even as they voted to examine the implications of the concept of prescribed duties, the delegates gave clear evidence that they were not yet ready to move ahead: this study must be "within the context of the informed choice so precious to Reform Judaism." Ordained duties, mitzvot, and informed choice are mutually exclusive terms. Reform will not be able to build a vibrant movement it if keeps insisting that each person not only can but must decide not only how active they will be as Jews but what constitutes a Jewish way of life.

Small groups of the spiritually engaged exist in all our congregations, and there is a lot of talk among rabbis about building on such groups. A recent article by Harvey Fields in the Journal of Reform Judaism put it this way: "We need to stop counting the house and begin paying attention to how we can create a sharing worship community. How shall we create such a community? By building it patiently, lovingly, person by person." But the question remains: What model has Reform in mind to guide this work? What cluster of ideas will be promulgated and accepted as redemptive? A building needs blueprints, and this community needs the will to work through the many challenges it must meet before it will be able to transform itself from what is today essentially a community of fate into a community of faith.

The Reform Jewish community is by no means inert. Our congregations are full of activity, some of which is clearly focused on religious concerns. The young have shul-ins. Young parents arrange Sabbath dinners to learn the songs and the blessings which they can share with their children. Families go on retreats which discuss the question, "How to Jew"--using "Jew" as a verb. In one synagogue you will find a small group of Reform Jews meeting for daily worship. In another a few regulars meet weekly to go over texts. Some rabbis are finally beginning to listen to those who for years have complained that all the hubbub around life-cycle activities on Friday night denies them the satisfaction of Sabbath worship. A few congregants are even beginning to see their rabbi as a spiritual guide rather than as congregational factotum and general counselor. But it is also clear that the many years during which Reform tended to treat the issues of religion offhandedly have dulled the synagogue's sensibilities. Congregational leaders are often chosen for their ability, and many accept these responsibilities out of a sense of nobles oblige rather than out of personal conviction. The practical people who are in positions of leadership tend to believe a congregation should emphasize what people "want."

Michael Meyer has written:

> From its very beginning the Reform Movement had drawn a great many Jews for whom religion, in some cases Jewishness, was distinctively peripheral to their lives. They attended synagogue rarely, having joined for reasons of respectability and their children's identity. Many, especially in the larger cities, were not desirous of deeper involvement. They were content to come to the temple for the High Holy Days or for the celebration of life cycle events. At present this segment tends to see the rabbi as more of a priest who officiates on special occasions than a spiritual or moral guide, while, for their part, the rabbinical and lay leaders are now rarely imbued with that effervescent self-confidence which had done battle with apathy in an earlier age.

Although I largely agree with this late 1970s analysis, I am not convinced that lethargy or lack of confidence are now, or were then, the hallmarks of the rabbinate or of congregational leadership. If anything, there has been a kind of frenetic energy within the Movement. Hundreds of what are inappropriately called "creative services" have been pasted up and Xeroxed. Congregations plunged into the Havurah movement until they discovered that these self-help groups were successful in the centers of alienation—the Valley outside Los Angeles for example—but not in such relatively stable communities as Cleveland. Our schools are always experimenting with new curricular materials. Our kids go to Israel and NFTY camps and at conclave time descend on the host congregation like cheerful locusts. The problem has not been, and is not, a lack of institutional activity, but the fact that Reform did not challenge the predominantly secular attitudes of third-generation American Jews or place before them in an effective way the need for spiritual commitments and disciplines. The results are everywhere to be seen. Reform is rich in buildings, numerically strong, able to look back on some fine accomplishments, but unclear in its policies and uncertain of the future. Reform's old cluster of redemptive ideas has clearly lost much of its effectiveness, but a compelling new focus has not been found. To find that center, to work out ways to awaken this generation of American Jews to the fact that they—we—desperately need the encouragement and guidance of a warm and satisfying religious life, that is the challenge. I am convinced our physicians have diagnosed what is causing our spiritual deficiency which is at the root of our problems. Unfortunately, I am not fully convinced major segments of the community care enough about their spiritual health to accept the prescribed regimen.

TEACHING JUDAISM IN THAILAND

Richard G. Marks
Mahidol University

For the past three years I have been teaching Judaism in
Bangkok, Thailand, at Mahidol University, to graduate
students, all of whom are Buddhist. They study Judaism as one
of the required subjects in a graduate program of comparative
religion that requires them also to study the other major
religious traditions. I was invited to join the program by
its founder and director, Dr. Pinit Ratanakul, for the
principal reason that Judaism, as one significant religion of
the world, simply merited inclusion in the curriculum; there
was the further and not inconsequential factor that funding
could be found from abroad.

When I asked the students why they were studying
comparative religion, they gave a variety of reasons--to learn
how other religions foster happiness and peace and to bring
these ideas into Thai society for its improvement, or to
promote tolerance among people, or to seek truth or understand
"religion," or, most interesting to me, a Buddhist idea of
"acquiring merit" (dai kusol),[1] that we elevate or purify
ourselves a little whenever we vanquish a portion of our
ignorance. As for myself, I wanted to leave my book-filled
office and see a part of Asia, to meet people whose culture
and religion are very different from my own, and to gain a new
perspective upon the Judaism I had been studying in Los
Angeles.

In this essay I shall describe what occurred as my
students and I attempted to vanquish a little of our
ignorance. Our experience provides, I think, some insight
into the religion of Thai university students, an interesting
perspective upon traditional Judaism, and an example of the
questions and problems that may arise in teaching a religious
tradition to people whose own religion is very different.

I shall begin by presenting a picture of the students and
the world of thought out of which they looked at Judaism. I
shall then describe a little of what they saw in the Judaism
they studied--both their initial perceptions and the ideas
they later formed of the aspects of Judaism they considered
most difficult to understand. This description of the
students and their perceptions of Judaism comprise the first
two parts of this essay; the rest of the essay, parts 3 and 4,
intended as commentary upon those perceptions, considers

questions, both specific and general, that arose in the
pursuit of cross-cultural understandings. I shall explore in
detail one of the specific problems that complicated my
students' perceptions of Judaism--the problem of understanding
"holiness" in Judaism; and shall then discuss my own role in
Thailand as an interpreter of a foreign religion, concluding
the essay with reflections upon one underlying problem that
seems to inhere in all our endeavors to understand different
cultures and religions.

1

My students during those two years were fourteen graduates
whose ages ranged mostly from twenty-two to thirty-two, with a
few older than this. They always behaved toward me with
kindness and respect, treating me as their <u>khru</u> (revered
teacher). When teachers enter the classroom, students make
the gesture of respect called a <u>wai</u>, bowing their heads while
holding their hands, palms pressed together, before their
faces. It will be the shy affectionate smiles of my students
that I shall remember, their thoughtful solicitude toward me,
and the modesty and trust with which they spoke their views.

As much as possible in this essay I allow the students to
speak through their own words, which I copy either from papers
they wrote or from notes I made in classroom or office. They
have granted me their (amused) permission to do so and have
read everything I am writing about them. I alter only their
grammar on occasion to make their English read more
smoothly.[2]

Let us listen first to some rather personal statements
they wrote in response to two questions about their religious
values.

> I am a Buddhist; I pay respect to the Buddha. . . . I
> believe in the result of virtue, that it will bring me
> success in life, and when I die, I shall be reborn in a
> better status.

> I pay respect to the image of the Buddha and everything
> that is related to him, such as his relics, his words in
> the Tripitaka, and his disciples. . . . I say a prayer
> before going to bed. I sacrifice food to my ancestors on
> special days many times a year. I give food to the monks
> in the morning.

> The story of the Buddha is very important to me, because
> Lord Buddha is the primary example for me to follow. . . .
> He knows and understands the meaning of life and how to
> reach Nirvana.

> As a Buddhist my highest reverence is for the Triple Gem,
> <u>Ratanattaya</u>--that is, the Buddha, the Dhamma [his
> teachings], and the Sangha [the monastic order]. . . . In

my house there are many Buddha-images, a set of Tripitaka, and images of some reverend monks. The stories of the Buddha and his disciples are the guidepoints in my life. These stories tell me how I should live and what is the goal of life. They inspire me when I encounter obstacles.

I follow the basic Dhamma by not doing evil, increasing good, and purifying my mind, in order to receive happiness in my life. . . . For example, I do good by giving money to the poor, offering food to monks, following the Precepts, trying to meditate whenever it is possible, and listening to explanations of the doctrine. For purifying my mind, I try not to cause suffering to others, and I try to excuse anyone who makes me unhappy so that I do not keep sins in my mind. . . . Before I go to bed, I always chant in Pali the words, 'Praise to the Buddha, the Holy One, Perfect in Wisdom.'

Then there were two students who expressed a more questioning attitude toward some portions of Buddhist doctrine.

I am a Buddhist, but I am hardly religious. . . . I do help people whom I think deserve pity: giving money to some needy person, taking care of children or old people. Is that called 'doing good'? I am not sure. . . . The story of the Buddha is not the most important to me because his life is different from mine, an ordinary woman. . . I have some hope of reaching Nirvana in the very far future [after many rebirths]. But my own business is the most important concern in my life.

My highest concern may be safety, nirvana, social status, or whatever is suitable for me . . . depending on reasoning, time, place, and necessity. One night my mother, who died eighteen years ago, inhabited my father in order to visit her children. . . . and to perform the wedding ceremony for me. This event is strange but true; I did not know it was possible.

These sentences open up to us significant aspects of the religious world of my students. Thoughts, experiences, and symbols such as these were in their minds as they studied Judaism.

The particular interpretations of Buddhist tradition that my students voice, in the sentences just cited and in their ideas to be presented later in this essay, may be said to reflect in part the worldview of middle-class urbanites with a formal education. I hasten to add, however, that even among the fourteen students in my courses, there was a considerable divergence of opinion. Several students, for example, thought of nibbana as their life's goal, while most said this was impractical and suited only for monks. A number of students had been influenced in their articulation of Buddhist doctrine by the famous Thai monk, Baddhadasa Bhikkhu, whose contemporary reformulations of Buddhist doctrine are popular among university students (my student Twan lived for a time at this hermitage in the south); other students preferred more traditional interpretatons. Some students wore amulets, one was an experienced astrologer, another sought help from a brahman god; but most students expressed skepticism toward these practices. A few students took a stance intentionally outside of Buddhist doctrine and institutions.

"Reformed Buddhist worldview" is a phrase that the anthropologist Charles Keyes uses to identify the distinctive views of the Thai middle class. He uses the word "Reformed" because he traces the origin of these views to the educational reforms enacted by King Monghut and King Chulalongkorn in the nineteenth century, which replaced the traditional Thai cosmology with one more in accord with Western science. It is this worldview that is now being taught in Thai schools and, if only in broad outline, is reflected in the words of my students. Keyes suggests as its "salient features," besides the adoption of Western science, the tendencies to interpret kamma with an emphasis on moral action in the present and its future consequences (rather than the past as a determinant of the present), and to extend the means of "making merit" beyond its traditional religious setting and into the realm of daily life.[3] I present Keyes' generalizations to provide a context for my students' thought, but I must also note the presence of those of my students who question basic elements of this worldview. Even among middle-class Thai outside the universities I can discern a texture of thought much more complex than "reformed worldview" might suggest.

Specifically, the adoption of a reformed science-oriented worldview means the rejection of the classical Indian mythology, with its many worlds, gods, and orders of beings, which was the central feature of the traditional Thai world view (in the form seen most clearly in the fourteenth-century text, Traiphum Phraruang); also rejected, or seriously undermined, are the cosmos and cultus of powerful gods and spirits which derive from brahmanical and indigenous religious traditions--and indeed nearly all parts of what I shall later discuss as the realm of "the saksit" in Thai popular religion.[4] Thus, one of the assumptions underlying many of my students' ideas found in this essay is that Buddhist doctrines are fully consistent with Western science; another related assumption is that they can all be tested rigorously by reason and experience.[5] In regard to other religions, the students are concerned mainly with the religions' effectiveness in alleviating suffering and fostering moral behavior, the primary functions of religions; and to the students, suffering is the foremost problem of life. (I leave it to readers more knowledgeable than I to determine just how the thought of my students is related to the Pali canon and to Theravada tradition.)

Many of the rituals and symbols of my students' religion, as well as important doctrines, have appeared already in their personal statements, but a sense of its wholeness remains to be suggested before concluding this brief introduction to my students. I shall only sketch lightly what has impressed me over a period of time as being its central order and movement.

The central symbols, then, of their religion seem to be the Buddha together with kamma seen as a law of existence (and some students during my second year told me they think more often about kamma than about the Buddha). The Buddha seems to have significance as an extraordinary sage who sought and discovered the most important truth about life (Dhamma), truth that can alleviate suffering. Students often speak of suffering and problems on the one hand, contrasted to happiness and peace on the other. Suffering is alleviated basically by moral behavior, unpossessiveness (detachment) and contentment, a calm mind, and a realization of the inherent impermanence and incompleteness of life. Kamma holds significance as an essential structure of life, its moral nature, a force sustaining moral bahavior; bad behavior inexorably results in bad kamma, variously conceived as internal, interpersonal, social, or material suffering. nibbana has no important role in the life of most of my students, although it might be said to be present indirectly in the detachment and calm which all the students seek. When I asked them what was the most important teaching of Buddhism, they would most often answer with a sentence from the Dhammapada (183): "To do good, to refrain from evil, and to purify the mind." (This sentence appears twice in the students' writings included in this essay.) I was struck throughout by the lighthearted tone, the gentleness and modesty, with which all of this was expressed.[6]

2

Judaism is hardly known at all in Thailand. When I say "Jewish Religion" (sasana yiw) to people outside the university, they are totally puzzled, although they are familiar with sasana i-salam (Islam) and sasana khrit (Christianity). In comparitive religion courses (of which there are a growing number), Judaism, if even mentioned, is described as the foundation of Christianity, and so is relegated to the "Old Testament." This is how Judaism was presented at Mahidol University when taught by a Catholic priest just before my arrival. Jews, on the other hand, have a definite reputation in Thailand--a reputation mixed partly of the greedy Shylock of Merchant of Venice, which all Thai schoolchildren are required to read in translation, and partly of Einstein, Entebbe, Moshe Dayan, and Israelis turning deserts into farmlands. In the Thai language the word "Jew" is synonymous with "miserly, greedy," and my students once told me that this was the way they had expected me to behave. Yet many Thai admire Israelis for their courage, cleverness, and austerity, and upon my arrival at Mahidol, a number of people there asked me to explain how Judaism had made Israel strong and enabled American Jews to acquire so much wealth and political power. News of recent events in Lebanon, however, has resulted in a worse impression of "the Jewish state" and "the Jewish army"--as the Thai-language newspapers call them.

In my course on the History of Judaism, I lectured first on the Biblical and rabbinic history of the religion, and then presented traditional Judaism in its classical rabbinic and prayerbook forms through the structure of its central symbols, which, like many others before me, I took to be Torah, Israel, and God (and religious life ordered through sacred times, places, and actions). I spoke afterwards about modern history and modifications of the traditional structure. In the second semester I participated in a seminar in which five religions were studied in relation to five philosohical categories--human nature, salvation, ultimate reality, knowledge, and religious life (somewhat a Buddhist sequence of topics).[7]

If my students knew nothing of Judaism, they had nevertheless acquired a familiarity, however vague, with Muslim and Christian doctrines, and had encountered Christian missionaries. Presented then with Judaism, the students tended to place it in the same category, and I think their previously-formed impressions of Islam and Christianity influenced to an extent their responses to Judaism.

Thus, when toward the beginning of my course, while we were studying the Bible, I asked the students what the word, "God" meant to them, they were fully prepared with answers. The topic was clearly not new to them. One student told me that she considered God to be "very nonsense," because the law of kamma explains life fully without God. Another student, Arastum, asserted that God is a socially-conditioned construct, functioning mainly to lend authority to laws and moral codes. Twan said that he thought of God as nature, the totality of the universe. I asked him, "When the Bible says that God spoke to Abraham, what does that meant to you?" Twan replied, "It means that Abraham learned from nature." Finally, Voradej, the student with the greatest formal knowledge of Buddhist doctrine and literature, said that Buddhists simply have no need for "the gods" and should rely only upon themselves for salvation, as the Buddha taught. My second group of students expressed similar ideas but preferred psychological interpretations. One student, for example, asserted that what people call God is really a consciousness of the good and real; she added, somewhat inconsistently, that the prophets had discoverd goodness and reality, Dhamma, but identified it with the will of God in order to gain acceptance.

It was also during the initial stages of the course that the students presented me in their papers with some surprising interpretations of Jewish literature. I had asked them to explain a number of rabbinic sayings in Pirqei Avot (Chapters of the Fathers, a part of the Mishnah). Twan chose to interpret the statement attributed to Antigonos of Sokho, "Do not be like servants who serve the master [God] for the sake of a reward." Twan explained this as a description of the true meaning of generosity (dana in Pali, than in Thai—one of the five Ennobling Virtues): "Giving without taking back (rewards) is the real merit"—thanamai, merit gained through giving.[8] Voradej, in his delightful scholastic style, explained Avot 2.13 (the story of Yohanan ben Zakkai sending his students to find "the best path for a person to follow," the answer being lev tov, a good heart): "Rabbi Yohanan taught that a good heart was the essence of all good actions. Action and words are manifestations of mind. A man with a good mind is a generous man." (This story from Avot thus bears a partial resemblance to a Buddhist teaching to which many Thai refer, that the mind is the most important determinant of behavior and experience, and hence must be purified in order that life be seen truly and suffering reduced.) In the student newsletter, Voradej chose two statements from Avot to translate, one of which was Ben Zoma's dictum (4.1) containing the words, "Who is [truly] strong? He who conquers his passions (yizro)"—easily a Buddhist teaching. (Indeed, compare the Dhammapada, 103-104.) Arastum interpreted a group of statements attributed to Hillel (Avot 2.5). "Do not be sure of yourself until the day of your death" meant to her that we cannot depend on anything in life because "everything is changing all the time," is impermanent, anicca. Finally, Sriphen recognized the law of Kamma in Hillel's words addressed to a skull floating in the water: "Because you drowned others, others have drowned you; and in the end, those who drowned you will themselves be drowned" (2.7). These interpretations from my students are fascinating examples of the probably universal tendency to perceive the foreign through the familiar--perhaps the central theme of this essay.

After explaining as best I could the process of midrash, the characteristic rabbinic method of discovering new meaning in scripture, I asked the students to write midrash of their own (minus the traditional hermeneutic rules) that would be personally meaningful to them. I told them that, so long as they understood the literal meaning in the Bible, I would not mind reading Buddhist interpretations. Here are some examples, then, of Thai midrash:

> On Leviticus 19:14, "You shall not curse the deaf or put an obstacle before the blind," Parichart wrote, "Everyone possesses his own karma. The deaf and blind are so because of past actions. Good Buddhists will not add to the pain of these people--which would bring bad karma. Instead, we should let the example of their suffering encourage us to follow the teachings of the Buddha."

> On Leviticus 7:26-27, "You shall eat no blood whatever, whether of bird or animal. . . whoever eats any blood will be cut off from his people," Twan, after correctly explaining the literal meaning, offered two exegeses, both based upon the Buddhist prohibition of destroying life. "Do not," he wrote, "earn your living on the suffering of others, whether of birds or animals, including man" (referring to right livelihood, samma ajiva, which means not to earn a living from trade in weapons, slavery, liquor, drugs, or meats--as a hunter or butcher), and then a political interpretation: "If you exploit the poor [birds and animals] too much, you will be overthrown [cut off] by the people, as with the Shah of Iran."

> Arastum, combining exegesis with overt comparison, suggested a similarity between the Buddhist path to Nibbana and the "hill of the Lord" in Psalm 24:3-4: "Who will ascend the hill of the Lord. . . ? He who has clean hands and a pure heart. . . ." She wrote, "We must avoid bad thoughts and bad action, and if we do, we shall see God. God in this meaning is a condition, the condition without evil in our mind. 'The hill of the Lord' means the way to attain this condition. Nirvana in Buddhism is also a condition, one attained by doing good, not doing bad, and purifyng the mind, because everything changes continuously and passes away. To have a pure mind is to understand this condition of no-self [anatta] profoundly and to get rid of passion, which is caused by clinging to 'self.' In Judaism a pure heart means no evil in the

mind, which is different from the pure heart or mind of Buddhism."

The same student, always a copious writer, offered a political exegesis of the same verse: "'Clean hands and pure heart' mean that politicians and officials in Thailand must have good action and good thought. They should not use intrigue, corruption, or murder, or use their power in the wrong way, to raise their rank and salary . . . The way to higher rank and salary that is the way of God comes from goodness and not from doing evil."

The preceding comments and writings of the students come from the early weeks of the first course I taught on the history of Judaism. Then at the end of this course, I used part of the final exam to ask students to name those aspects of Judaism that they thought were the most difficult for a Thai to understand. The answers to this question, based on a greater familarity with the subject, give the clearest indication of what Judaism looked like within the cultural setting of urban Thailand.

Almost all the students said that the interest of Jews in God was difficult to understand. Voradej explained this by the absence among Thai Buddhists of any similar "concept" and interest in it. The closest belief, he said, is the belief in thewada (devata in Pali), powerful superhuman beings consisting of "soul and subtle body" who enjoy more pleasure than human beings do, but also suffer pain and fight among themselves. Thai people turn to thewada for help in solving practical problems such as illness, misfortune, or evil spells. (Voradej is describing semi-divine beings which are part of the classical Indian or brahmanical cosmology that remains a central feature of popular religion in Thailand. This realm of "the saksit," within which thewada belong, will be discussed further in Part 3.) As an example of a thewada, Voradej named the Four-Faced Brahma whose image is located at the Erawan Hotel (although other Thai classify Brahma as a thep, implying a god higher than a thewada). Many people come to this powerful image to ask the god for help, in return for which they promise to give wooden elephants, dance performances, or make donations to a hospital fund. Voradej was suggesting that it is this kind of god that enters the minds of Thai Buddhists when they hear Jews, Muslims and Christians speak of their god.

Another student offered the same observation, and when I asked him how the God of Judaism differs, he replied that the God in Judaism has unlimited power, whereas the brahmanical Gods are limited. Apparently, then, this student himself thought of the God of Judaism basically in the image of a magnified thewada. Two other students described God similarly, as "the greatest," having "great power," "enormous power."

Another difficult aspect of Judaism, according to the students, was the meaning that Torah, as revelation, has for Jews. For Theravada Buddhists, the important knowledge in life is Dhamma, which is knowledge about the structure of reality and how to alleviate suffering and attain Nibbana. Some Thai Buddhists use the English word "nature" in reference to the reality known through Dhamma (for example, Buddhadasa and the teacher-writer Phra Rajavaramuni), sometimes implying through this word a distinction between "natural" and "supernatural." Most of my students defined "natural" in a manner not very different from Western positive science. They would say that Dhamma was discoverd by the Buddha through observaton and reasoning "within nature." Hence, as Voradej phrased it, truth for Buddhists "is not revealed but discovered," and so the notion that truth should come from beyond "nature" seemed strange. Furthermore, whereas Dhamma is knowledge of the laws of reality, "it seems peculiar to a Thai for a Being to make a law [Torah] apart from reality." This again was Voradej speaking.

Earlier in the course I had asked students to compare Dhamma with Torah, and the chief difference upon which the students focused was in the source of knowledge--that Dhamma comes from within the "natural" world and Torah from outside, from a God that they conceived as being supernatural. From this distinction the students derived all others. Torah appeared to be a law imposed upon human life which Jews were compelled (unnaturally) to obey, whereas Dhamma was knowledge and a way of life which people would choose out of a natural concern to lessen suffering. Several students expressed the opinion that Jews obey Torah out of faith, but Buddhists follow Dhamma out of rational examination and decision. "Buddhists feel respect for the Dhamma because it is the best way to live . . . but Jews and Christians feel respect for their scriptures because the scriptures are the word of God, which they must have faith in." Thus, Buddhists learn Dhamma "by wisdom" (that is, rational thought), whereas "Jews study Torah by faith" and "should not criticize or hesitate to believe." Twan, the author of this last statement, goes on to cite the Kalamas Sutta, which in his mind means that "the Buddhist feels free to doubt until it is clear enough to accept or believe. This is what I feel is quite different from religions that have God."[9] (The students remained convinced throughout the course that knowledge of God could never derive from rational inquiry, personal prayer, or historical experience.)

Two Jewish doctrines identified as being troublesome were those of election and Israel's convenant with God. I had had the students read a portion of Henri Dumery's Phenomenology and Religion, in which these doctrines are interpreted as expressions of a historical mode of perceiving "the Absolute" whereby particularistic Jewish history acquires a universalistic function as a medium of revelation for the benefit of mankind.[10] But a number of students continued to hear the doctrines as expressions of an attitude of national superiority or egoism (of which the students disapproved) or even, according to Nanta, a deep love for ancestors (which she considers worthy). Many of the Thai I have met are proud of their tolerance toward other religions, and my students will assert that all religions are good for those who practice them, or that all religions teach ultimately the same truths. Hence, for one people to claim that its prophets and history reveal truths in a special way, more fully than do other religions, is to be intolerably "biased," as one student termed it.

The laws of the Torah appeared "strict" to many students, and they had trouble finding any value in the harsh life that they imagined in Judaism. According to Nongyao, Buddhists have no strict obligatory laws; people practice Dhamma because it appears good or useful to them, and disobedience is consequently not a sin. Nongyao concluded, therefore, that Buddhists have more freedom than Jews; she said that Buddhists could, for example, kill an animal if they had good reasons, even though this transgressed one of the fundamental Five Precepts.

I had interpreted Jewish ritual as symbolical acts of connecting one's life with God. Voradej thought that Thai people would consider all these ritual actions a difficult way of life, asking, "Why would anyone try always to connect his life to God's will?" According to Voradej, "most Thai live without a sense of connection with the Dhamma or anything sacred," and so they would ask a similar question about the life of a Buddhist monk. "But a pious Buddhist would understand the Jewish attempt at sanctification." (Here Voradej draws a distinction between those Thai who feel little interest in Buddhism and those who are "pious Buddhists," supposing the two groups to react differently toward traditional Judaism.)

Two of the students thought that the Jewish interest in history as a realm of sacred events was difficult to understand, because, they said, history, except for the life of the Buddha, is not important to Buddhists.

We return, finally, to the subject of "faith," which the students had mentioned in connection with Torah. Three of the students told me that the importance of faith in Judaism made the religion difficult for a Buddhist to understand, since (in the view of these students) faith is unimportant in Buddhism. Twan defined "faith" as a belief that cannot be proved through reason and experience. The problem was that "if I know that God doesn't exist, how can I understand Judaism?" Twan's solution was to "begin by imagining faith, such as the belief in God, and then I can understand the rest of Judaism." Upon being questioned, Twan acknowledged that faith may be part of Buddhism, but faith comes at the end, after a person has tested the truth of the Dhamma, whereas in Judaism faith must precede all else, since the basic doctrines cannot be proved. (Twan's definition of faith fits well with the positivistic science-oriented worldview of my students, although it may also be vaguely connected with doctrines in the Pali canon.) Sumadhya expressed the same idea about the precedence of faith in Judaism: "first come obedience, worship, and faith," she said, "and then activity follows." Amnat, too, pointed to faith as constituting an essential difference betwen Judaism and Buddhism. "Buddhists," he said, "have a rational religion, and Judaism is a traditional religion, emphasizing faith and obedience. First Jews believe, and then they find reasons." According to Sumadhya, in Judaism the knowledge is "sacred," deriving from God, but in Buddhism the knowledge is "rational," deriving from insight: "If you prove the Dhamma is real, you follow it."

I myself had never used the word "faith" in speaking of Judaism, and I repeatedly argued against the students' conclusions. In the second semester I wrote a brief essay in which I questioned the validity of their definition of faith. I argued that by their definition, every religion is "faith," including Buddhism, because it too is based upon certain fundamental assumptions or interpretations of reality which are unprovable or precede reason and experience. I therefore suggested that the term "faith" be applied only to the act of holding beliefs which are consciously thought to oppose, surpass, or to be undemonstrated by reason and normal experience.[11] For most Jews over the span of Jewish history, the relationship with God was not based on faith because they did not consider their knowledge of ultimate things to be particularly unreasonable or problematic.

In response to this essay, the students, led by Voradej, assured me that they considered faith an admirable quality in Judaism, and they asserted that faith has an important role in Buddhism. The first act of a Buddhist, before he or she can even begin to follow the path of purification and insight, is an act of faith, saddha, in which he or she accepts as true, unproven, the reality of the Buddha's enlightenment and the actuality of the law of kamma. Later, after practising Dhamma and reflecting upon it, the Buddhist is expected to be able to prove by experience the truth of these foundational assumptions which had been initially accepted on faith.

Thus the students had adopted my definition of faith and then set it neatly into their former picture of a fully demonstrable Buddhism and an unattested Judaism! Perhaps they were right.

Contrary to the other students, Parichart asserted that Judaism would not be difficult for Thai people to understand. She based this opinion upon her belief that many Thai people have "compromised" by embracing parts of religions other than Buddhism--particularly Brahmanism and the cultus of local spirits. These religions (and not Buddhism), she thinks, provide an adequate basis for understanding the role of God in Judaism. As she explains it, many Thai people think there are supernatural powers that control events within limited localities. The God of Judaism is like these gods or spirits except that he is "transcendent and unlimited" in his "power to create and act." I asked Parichart to explain further the differences betwen the local gods revered in Thailand and the god revered in Judaism. "There are many gods," she replied, "but they do not reveal the truth about life. They want offerings of incense and flowers. Only if people make an offering will the gods help them. But in Judaism there is only one god. He reveals his will. He is connected with everything in human life. He does not want offerings; he wants practice in accord with Torah." Then I challenged Parichart to prove to me that the God of Judaism is not difficult to understand, and she added the following thoughts: "God rules over all nations. He chose Israel, revealed his will to Abraham and Israel. According to Dumery, God wants Israel to represent and spread Judaism to all the world. God is righteous: he punishes the wicked and rewards the good. God is the supreme authority. He is creator and redeemer. He saves mankind, as in the history of Israel and he will send the Messiah."

Such, then, are some of the replies given to my question. The students expressed these opinions after having read selections from many of the standard introductory texts in Judaic Studies (writings of Neusner, Steinberg, Lipman, Werblowsky, Donin, and Kaufman, to name a few), as well as numerous prayers from the prayerbook, and a few selections from the classical literature; the students, then, were speaking out of a knowledge of Judaism, although their comprehension of it can indeed be faulted. The student writings cited from the beginning of the course, especially the midrash, emphasized similarities between Judaism and the students' own religion, whereas the opinions cited from the end of the course, because of the nature of the question itself--what in Judaism is difficult to understand?--necessarily stressed differences. Although the answers may sound critical of Judaism, criticism was not their intention; rather, it was I who had elicited these responses because I was interested in learning more clearly how Judaism was perceived, and especially the differences that were perceived.

One particular student, after reading the foregoing opinions expressed by the other students, voiced her concern lest I and my readers interpret the opinions as criticism. This student, Mrs. Nanta ("Mrs." because she is married), a kind and sincere woman of middle age, pious and observant in her Buddhism, is an instructor preparing to introduce a comparative religion curriculum at a teachers' college in a neighboring province. She wanted to assure me that she believes that all religions are good; and she also thought she understood why Jews revere God. Her idea is, in brief, that God is an abstract phenomenon which, like kamma, people experience but cannot fully describe. "God is there, we feel God, but we cannot describe him fully." The experience of God seems to her to be related to the good or bad feelings experienced by people in consequence of the good or bad actions they have performed--a concept somewhat different from that of the conscience. These feelings, in Mrs. Nanta's view, are called "kamma" by Buddhists and "God" by Jews.

Mrs. Nanta's attempt to understand Jewish experiences of God resulted in transforming those experiences into her own experience of the effect of kamma, which, I think, touches only one aspect of what God has meant to Jews. Nevertheless, I should like to point out that her intention was to grant as much reality to Jewish experiences of God as she grants to her own experience of kamma. ("Kamma is abstract; we feel it but we can't tell exactly what it is.") And for Mrs. Nanta, the experience of kamma has ultimate significance in her life.

3

You may have been struck by a comparison that Sumadhya made between Torah and Dhamma. Torah, she said, was "sacred," since it came from God; Dhamma, however, was not sacred but "rational," having been discovered through human insight. Earlier in the semester, during a discussion in my office, Arastum had claimed even further that nothing in Buddhism was sacred, because Buddhism is part of the everyday world and available to all people. Torah, on the other hand, was sacred, because it came from outside the ordinary world. I countered with the best rationalistic definition of "sacred" that I could muster, suggesting that Lord Buddha might be extraordinary in some way, perhaps in his wisdom, and reminding her that she performs a krab (a gesture of respect, kneeling to touch head to floor three times) before addressing a monk. "Doesn't this mean that you consider the monk sacred?" Arastum replied that the Buddha was an ordinary man who merely had more wisdom than other people, and that monks are ordinary men, too, and hence not holy. "Buddhists respect all these," she said, "but we do not think they are sacred."

I recount this incident because it led to what became for me a lesson in the linguistic complexities--but also cultural and personal--in trying to speak and understand across cultures. It became a lesson in the deflective, skewing effect which language has upon our perception of the foreign. Eventually, because my students tended to perceive Judaism through the language and assumptions of their own culture (and I through my Reform Jewish upbringing), I was compelled to examine just how holiness in traditional Judaism relates to the Thai cultural forms familiar to my students.

After my conversation with Arastum, I noticed that some of the other students concurred with the way she categorized Buddhism and Judaism, and that, furthermore, they put Islam and Christianity into the same category as Judaism, the category of religions of "sacred" things. I noticed also that

the students used the word "sacred" in speaking of amulets and
the shrine of the Erawan Brahma, and this was my clue. After
a little investigation I realized that the students had been
relying upon their dictionaries' translation of the English
"sacred" into the Thai word, saksit. Saksit applies
principally to special objects and beings that are thought to
exert extraordinary power, such as images of Brahman gods,
certain Buddha images, and spirits residing in particular
trees and locales. These are saksit because they exert a
power that protects or otherwise affects human life by
mysterious means. Saksit thus denotes the quality of
possessing such power.[12]

Hence, if the students looked at Judaism as a religion of
saksit phenomena--because God is not wholly of the ordinary
world, Torah comes from God, Jews pray constantly to God, and
Jewish history tells of extraordinary events--then the
students would see Torah as an object of power and Jewish life
as primarily a pursuit of power. Indeed, Sriphen once wrote,
"The goal of living with God is to gain the sudden advantage.
Isn't this a characteristic of magic, not religion?"[13]
Sriphen apparently saw much of Jewish life, in contrast to her
notion of Buddhism, as a pursuit of "magical" power, aptly
defined as "the sudden advantage," and I think she had in mind
certain petitionary prayers from the prayerbook, as well as
Jacob Neusner's persuasive demonstration in The Way of Torah
of the importance of messianic redemption as a fundamental
orientation of traditional Jewish practice, prayer, and study.

Allow me to elaborate a little on the meaning of this word
saksit by which the students characterized Judaism.[14] As
the word is popularly used in everyday Thai life, at least in
Bangkok, it can apply to both objects and persons. One object
that is considered saksit mak (very saksit) is an image of a
giant named Thaohiran, built by King Rama VI after seeing the
giant in a dream. At the completion of the image, the spirit
of the giant was invited to dwell within the image, so that
the image is the actual dwelling of the giant and not merely a
symbol. Today the image is located on the grounds of Phra
Mongkut Hospital, and patients regularly come to it (or him)
to ask to be healed. A few of the many other objects in
Bangkok that are very saksit are the spirithouse of the
brother of Rama V (a spirit-house is a miniature house or
temple where the spirit-lord of a locale dwells and is offered
food and flowers by human beings), the Emerald Buddha, the
City Pillar, and, of course, the Brahma at the Erawan Hotel.

In each case, the object is thought to be the actual dwelling place of a powerful spirit, and the spirit's presence is what makes the object saksit. But even a simple tree may become saksit if people think that a spirit lives in it, and then its grounds become a place for revering the spirit and asking the spirit's help.

As for saksit persons, one example is the now deceased Acharya Khlai, a monk who lived in southern Thailand. It is said that he could bring rain, heal the sick, tell the future, and protect people from injury. He chanted mantras over coins and gave them to people for protection against all evils. One of the lecturers in my department wears on a chain around her neck the image of another saksit monk, and when she was involved in a serious automobile accident and escaped with only a minor cut, some of her friends concluded that the image had saved her life. If a person wants to gain access to greater power than a monk can offer, or wants to obtain illicit results (since monks and gods do not accede to immoral requests), the person can turn to a Mor Sa-ne, a "doctor of charms," or to a Mor Phi, a "doctor of ghosts." The former offers spells and potions, while the latter "cultivates" ghosts and sends them on errands of destruction against a client's enemies.[15]

This brief and over simple picture of saksit phenomena provides at least a rough indication of what was in the minds of my students when they associated the word saksit with Judaism. I must also add, however, that most of my students do not believe that saksit objects and people actually have the powers reputed to them, and that the students generally consider saksit power to be "supernatural" and the belief in its reality to be superstitious and irrational.[16] Yet a few of my students do seek help from saksit power. One of them, for example, sought the help of the Erawan Brahma in passing my exam, offering him in return three dozen boiled eggs (and then performed unexpectedly well on the exam). Some of the new students entering during this my third year brought to class an array of amulets, some very expensive, when they sat for a difficult English exam. Nevertheless, most of my students continue to adhere basically to the worldview of orthodox Western science, and even those who seek help from saksit power express doubts about its reality.

I was already somewhat acquainted with the word saksit when I learned that my students were applying it to the Torah and Sabbath as a translation of the English adjective "holy.

"My reaction was immediately to reject this translation and to draw a sharp line between Judaism and all saksit things. I did this thinking the question merited litle reflection, and feeling certain that kedushah in rabbinic literature and the prayerbook had no primary connection with power. But there was another reason for my reaction, a reason which I recognized only much later and only upon going home for a visit and hearing comments from some of my colleagues. I can see now that I felt a definite distaste for saksit objects and practices (yet distaste mixed with fascination), and I simply did not want my own religion placed in the same category. Occasionally, over the semester, I did point to certain parallels between the brahmanical gods and the god of Judaism, but I took pains also to distinguish the Jewish experience of God and to show that there was more to this god than the enormous power that students saw foremost in him, and Parichart, in her words recorded in the second part of this article, drew the kinds of distinctions that I had hoped the students would draw (even though many did not). Furthermore, I did not want the students dismissing Judaism in the way they dismissed the cults of saksit power for being eerie and "supernatural." If they were going to relate Judaism to phenomena in their own environment, as seemed inevitable, I preferred that they compare Judaism first with the disciplines and moral teachings of Buddhism.

In such way, personal feelings affect translation. I shall say more about this later, but here I should like to explore further the relationship between kedushah and the saksit. What do I reply to the next Thai student who asks me (as one already has this third year), "Is kadosh like saksit?" The question is difficult to answer not only because I must understand what the word saksit means to the student, but also because kadosh itself has varying meanings and references that defy any simple generalization.

Since saksit refers foremost to wondrous power, I must first ask what connection kedushah bears to power--and power not so much in the broad sense underlying G. van der Leeuw's conception of religion, according to which everything religious is "man seeking power in life," but power in the specific sense of "wondrous works."[17] In the traditional Jewish prayerbook, to which I limit my discussion here, kedushah clearly has no primary reference to power (which has its own term, gevurah). The kedushah of God, in accord with the word's cultic context, refers foremost to God's being utterly apart from and beyond the ordinary things of life (in the sense of Otto's term "wholly Other"), as in Ex. 15:11, Isa. 6:3, and the Kaddish prayer, all of these appearing prominently in the prayerbook. Holiness is also a positive ascription, speaking not merely of transcendence but of transcendent worth totally beyond all human ability to praise, as we find particularly in the Kaddish and the Kedushah, and in the Titbarakh and Atah Kadosh, which tell of angels, themselves holy and pure, declaring the higher holiness of God.[18]

Nevertheless, kedushah, though not itself power, is often connected or associated with power in important ways--kedushah being perhaps revealed or manifested, or perhaps upheld, through God's power. The Mikhamokha prayer, which is Ex. 15:11, connects God's holiness with his wondrous acts of redemption, oseh feleh (performing wonders) both in redeeming Israel from Egypt and, by association with the Ezrat Avotenu that precedes it, in daily acts of raising the lowly, freeing the captive, and helping the poor. These redemptive acts manifest a high and glorious power, and elicit from the congregation awe and praise: "Who is like You, majestic in holiness, awesome in praiseworthy deeds, performing wonders?" Indeed, numerous prayers connect God's holiness with his majesty, glory, and greatness;[19] whatever else these words mean, they suggest also a kingly, awesome power.

On the other hand, perhaps as often in the prayerbook, holiness is associated with the commandments of the Torah, particularly the Sabbath, through which both Israel and God are sanctified. God sanctifies Israel by giving them holy commandments to fulfill; Israel sanctifies God by declaring his holiness and obeying his commandments.[20] The holiness of Sabbath, Torah, and Israel seems to have no direct association with any immediate practical power, and primarily suggests being connected with or dedicated to God, holiness therein assuming qualities of purity, righteousness, and being set apart.[21] Yet power is still involved in the holiness of the commandments, since the congregation may hope, as in a prayer from the Tahanun, that by leading a holy life they may arouse God's mercy, out of which he may protect and finally redeem the congregation.[22] Inquiring into the human response to God's holiness, we discover several kinds: awe or reverence (yir'ah), praise, joy, blessings and sanctification of God.[23]

In rabbinic literature, as shown in the studies of Solomon Schechter and George F. Moore, kedushah refers particularly to separateness from all that is impure, wicked, and profane. Kiddush Hashem, sanctifying God's name, is a rabbinic phrase denoting human actions that bear witness to God's holiness with exceptional devotion, as in extraordinary deeds of charity and in martyrdom for the sake of the holy commandments; no power is involved. However, in two tannaitic midrashim cited by Moore (II, 102-03), the Sifre Deuteronomy and the Mekhilta, God (in the words of the former) "works miracles and does mighty works for the purpose of hallowing his holy name in the world"; God's holiness, according to this, is demonstrated through the manifestation of his extraordinary power.[24]

The word saksit, however, refers foremost to power. But since people feel "awe" toward saksit beings (yamkreng and khaoropyamkreng, words not used with non-saksit Buddhist phenomena), the word saksit carries with it the connotation of this special conduct setting the saksit apart from the rest of life. It is in this connotation of saksit, and in the power surrounding God's holiness, that the two words intersect. Moreover, the power exerted by saksit beings can be called "redemptive," since it aids and protects devotees; and, with the higher of the saksit beings, it is often a moral power, so that saksit shares these associations, too, with kadosh. Most devotees of saksit beings, however, do not see them as being utterly apart from the profane, or of highest worth; highest worth, together with goodness and purity, and perhaps also a certain sense of "otherness," are located far more in Buddhist institutions oriented primarily toward Dhamma than in institutions, both within and without the temples, centering primarily upon saksit beings, although for most Thai the division between the two orientations is not so sharp as many of my students believe it to be.

This difference in attitudes toward saksit and non-saksit Buddhist objects is an important issue for the comparison of kadosh and saksit, but it was a difficult question to investigate; my answers, though I think them generally correct, are inexact and need much more substantiation. This is the problem of determining what a foreign culture reveres most highly. The persons I questioned, my "informants" if you will, at the university and also outside it, were certain that most "people" (which I take to mean chao ban, "ordinary people,") in Bangkok and the towns of central Thailand feel differently toward the two realms, but this difference was hard to put into words. My informants all agreed that the Buddha and Sangha are "higher" than saksit beings, but higher in what way? Acharya Ratree Maruktat, whose account is fairly representative of what others told me, phrased the difference in this manner: the Buddha, Dhamma, and Sangha are sasana (in this context teaching, truth, religion), whereas the Brahma is not sasana. People respect the Erawan Brahma, she explained, only in relation to receiving his help, and because he is powerful and may punish disrespect; in contrast, people respect Lord Buddha "sincerely (cingcai), without expecting anything" in return "because he is Lord Buddha."[25] Everyone must go to the temples to make merit, and one is "not a good Thai, not a good person," if one does not wai a Buddha image. But whether to wai the Brahma or go to him for help is a matter of individual and practical decision. Another acquaintance asserted that the Buddha is "high and pure," but saksit beings are useful or dangerous, and most people have little feeling about them. Niels Mulder, a sociologist who spent three years interviewing people in the city of Chienmgmai, generally agrees with these observations.[26] All of this leads me to think that the term saksit, though it connotes the awe due to wondrous power, misses important aspects of kedushah, and that some of those other aspects are to be found in expressions of reverence for the Buddha and Buddhist institutions.

What I have discovered, in brief, is this: that while there is no single word or phrase related to non-saksit Buddhist institutions that captures those aspects of kedushah missed by saksit (how could there be, when the religions are so different?), there nevertheless exist complex clusters of words, symbols, and gestures that express reverence toward Buddhist symbols and institutions, as well as toward gods and royalty, and, though certainly not "equivalent" to kedushah, serve some of the functions of sanctification, the recognition and distinction of the sacred. I am thus suggesting that these expressions of reverence point to a realm in Thai life that in certain contexts could properly bear the term "sacred," used in its broad Eliadean sense. Yet, even though reverence is indeed one of the several responses to kedushah found in the prayerbook, this in no way implies that what is revered in Thailand is equivalent to kedushah.

Among these expressions of reverence, there is, to begin with, a series of words that all indicate acts and feelings of reverence, each word varying, however, in intensity of feeling, associated images, and the objects revered, and also varying in connotation somewhat from speaker to speaker. Here are a few of the most important of such words: khaorop, to regard highly, revere; bucha (puja in Pali), to show reverence outwardly through offerings such as flowers; khaoropbucha, a compound word applying to many persons as its object--Lord Buddha, the king, parents--but not usually to saksit objects; thun, thert, and thertthun, to put someone above onself, look up to, hold in high esteem, applied generally to living persons; sakkara, to worship, make a pilgrimage to pay homage to by offering incense and flowers, used only with religious objects and places, including saksit objects; khaoropsakkara and sakkarabucha, to worship and revere, used especially with Buddha images and relics as the object, but also with the higher gods; and khaoropthertthunbucha, part of the royal vocabulary, used only in reference to royalty. Wai and krab are two specific gestures for showing respect, and as words have the meaning "to respect" and "revere." In relation to saksit beings, the most frequent words are naptheu, meaning "to respect" or "believe in" (which applies also to a great many other objects, including sasana, a particular religion), and krabwaibucha, referring particularly to the specific actions of expressing respect for saksit beings; both naptheu and krabwaibucha are lower and weaker than khaorop. With all these words, the prefix na may be added to indicate that someone is "worthy of" worship, reverence, and so forth. This group of words ascribes great worth to its objects and tends to set them apart from ordinary things in life, especially since most of the words are Pali or Sanskrit, although the division between the revered and the ordinary seems a rather gradual one.

Next, there is a series of words which, when placed before the names of people and objects, indicate great respect, importance, or distinction. A few of these words (in their Thai and not Pali form) are phra, phraracha, phramahaa, phracao, somdet, and si (sri. The prefix phra, for example, is placed before the names of the Triple Gem: Phraphuttacao ("Reverend" or "Excellent" Lord Buddha), Phrasong, Phratham. "Phra" (from the Pali word vara) is associated in particular with monks, royalty, gods, and objects of veneration, as in Phra, a monk (bhikkhu), Phraboromthat, a relic of the Buddha, Phrabiyamaharat, "Reverend Beloved Great King," an appellation of King Rama V, and Phraphumcaothi, a guardian spirit lord of a locale. The word phra always indicates great worth and radical distinction from the ordinary, creating a boundary between its object and the rest of the world.

Finally, the Thai language also contains a set of Pali and Sanskrit words which are used in place of key words in ordinary language when speaking of or addressing monks, and also a further order of Pali and Sanskrit words, even higher, for speaking of Lord Buddha, royalty, and the highest gods. These separate orders of words likewise set their objects apart from ordinary life, treating them thereby as a distinct order of existence meriting great reverence.

(The latest Thai translation of the Bible usually translates kadosh as borisut, meaning "pure" or "innocent." For Thai culture, however, borisut generally connotes being free of all desire and evil, and Lord Buddha and new-born infants are the usual examples that come to mind. Perhaps borisut is the best alternative possible in a single word, but it often distorts the Hebrew meaning, sometimes makes the biblical sentences nonsensical in their context, and does not escape adverse cultural connotations.[27])

Thus, it is in this direction of the complex forms by which Thai language expresses reverence for Buddhist institutions, royalty, and the highest gods that I would seek language that points to some of the meanings of kadosh missed by saksit and serves some of the functions of sanctification. I must note, however, that this comparison is limited solely to the relationship between the kadosh of the prayerbook and the saksit of popular Thai culture, a question arising out of a practical situation in teaching. Therefore, my comparison does not deal with corresponding levels of religious expression in the two cultures: I did not compare the prayerbook with Thai classical literature, religious treatises, or mantras and prayers, which might convey a more serious attitude toward the gods; nor did I compare Thai popular religiosity with popular religiosity found in Jewish cultures of the past, which might exhibit a sense of kedushah different from the prayerbook's and would be found to involve demons, dark forces of evil, powerful masters of the Good Name, and spirits and angels, all of which are related to holiness in one way or another.

If a student again asks whether kadosh is like saksit and I reply, "Yes, in some ways" and then suggest that he or she also consider certain ways by which the Thai language

expresses reverence for objects that are not saksit, I shall
do so not because I advocate cross-cultural "translation" as
such; it gives us the wrong picture of the religion being
translated and wrenches things out of their contexts.
Nevertheless, there is, I think, a usefulness in
cross-cultural comparisons at certain points in one's study,
to suggest by broad analogy the general direction of a foreign
expression, to discover one's own involvement at home in many
of the forms and feelings one sees abroad, and to integrate
into one's own life the knowledge one gains in studying
others. I, as one example, was forced to try to integrate the
word saksit, with all its uncompliant foreignness, into my
understanding of kedushah. I think that this is part of what
understanding means: it joins the foreign with what is
nearest at hand.

However, the reality of the differences was what impressed
me most in my groping inquiry into the Thai language. I
discovered anew how willful and refractory a language can be
in speaking of experiences outside its realm of cultural
history, and how subtle, varied, eloquent, and richly allusive
it can be in speaking of its own culture. Every word has its
particular cultural reference: saksit referring to local gods
and spirits, sakkarabucha to the offering of flowers before an
image, and the elevated royal vocabulary to the king, Lord
Buddha, and the gods (thus classed together). Clearly, the
kadosh of the prayerbook, with its own special context and
allusions, often opposed to those of the Thai expressions,
cannot mean what any of those expressions mean. As I was
teaching my courses on Judaism, my students were mentally
translating every word I spoke into Thai with all its specific
cultural references, and this no doubt reinforced their
tendency to assimilate Judaism into kamma-oriented Buddhism
and institutions of saksit powers, as appears in their
writings and conversatons earlier recorded.

Yet, though these differences are real, both the Buddhist
and the Judaic traditions claim a validity that crosses
cultural boundaries. What the Buddha taught is meant to apply
to all human beings, of any society, any language, and the God
of Jewish prayer, though revealing himself first to Israel,
rules over and sustains all his creation and may be served and
sanctified everywhere, by all peoples. This implies that what
is revered now in only one culture is intended to be known and
understood in all, and this in turn justifies the attempt to

penetrate the in-turned forms of a foreign religion in the hope of reaching insights which extend beyond that culture and into our own and open a space even in the familiar predisposing words of our language.

4

I have asked myself why I first dismissed the possibility of a connection between kedushah and power, and part of the answer apparently lies in my own reluctance to attribute any real power to God. I likewise discount the claims made for the miraculous powers of saksit beings. Hence, in these respects, my own worldview turns out to bear resemblances to that of my students. Moreover, I was trying to present accurately a religious tradition that my students viewed as being a rather blind faith in "the supernatural," yet I myself, though rejecting the students' definition of faith, personally doubted Judaism's traditional sources of knowledge. I, a hesistantly secular Jew, was speaking about traditional Judaism, and speaking to people who had rejected the traditional cosmology of their own religion in exchange for a Western scientific cosmology. The differences, therefore, were not only those between Jewish and Thai cultures, Jewish and Buddhist religions, but also between religious and secular standpoints, traditional and science-oriented cosmologies (if I may be forgiven the imprecise usage here).

From the particular problem of speaking about kedushah with Thai students, I should like now to discuss more generally my role of interpreting Judaism in Thailand, considered in relation both to my own experience as well as to some broader questions about understanding across different religions and cultures. In the comments that follow, I exaggerate or epitomize the events somewhat in order to bring out what seems to me essential to my observations; in actuality, what I shall describe was more ambiguous, gradated, and opaque, less abstractable in texture.

I thought that in order to say something useful about Judaism, I would have to learn about the values and thinking of my students, as well as gain at least a little knowledge about Thailand and Pali Buddhism. Therefore, I read books, and I did a lot of listening to the students. I asked them questions about themselves and their religion, and I asked them to draw comparisons with the subjects we were studying. I looked for their reactions as I spoke or we studied a text and for opinions that might show through their writings. I

began to notice which subjects aroused nods of agreement and
which turned the room politely silent; and I began to
recognize recurrent phrases, words, and ideas. As time went
on, I rephrased my own words and questions to reflect upon
their ideas, to imply comparisons with life in Thailand, or to
point to familiar examples. I also began to select readings
and lecture topics on issues that specifically interested or
disturbed my students.

Not surprisingly, I noticed that those elements of Judaism
that elicited the nods of agreement were the ones that seemed
outwardly to resemble Buddhist doctrines (such as kamma,
anicca, karuna) and to concur with Western science. The
students were drawn also to texts dealing with the inner life,
practical wisdom, and ethics, and to anything evidencing
universal concerns and tolerance for other religions. My
students preferred to look at Judaism as a series of concepts
and techniques, which is basically the way Buddhism was
presented to them, as a philosophy of life with arguments for
its usefulness. In the eyes of my students, concepts were a
higher form of religion than symbols, myths, and rituals,
which seemed somewhat materialistic or coarse by comparison.
Therefore, my particular method of presenting Judaism--as
history experienced and interpreted, as a fundamental symbol
structure revealed most fully in liturgy and ritual--probably
reinforced the students' impression of a Judaism that was
magical, tradition bound, and not open to reason. When I told
the creation story in Genesis, two of my students made jokes
about what they saw as the curious illogic of the narrative.
The Yozer prayer from the liturgy elicited another joke from
one of the same students ("Poor God! He must be tired. He
has to create day and create night all the time!"), and, in a
later class, drew open scorn from another student. The
relevant sentences from the prayer declare: "In mercy You
give light to the world and to those who dwell on it; in Your
goodness You renew the work of creation every day,
continuously." Hearing this, the student said, with unusual
candor (and I paraphrase), "This is absurd. How can God
create the world every day? Everyone knows that the world
follows laws of nature. The world is impermanent. It always
changes." (To which I replied, "That is why God must sustain
the world at all times," and a student also defended the
prayer. I must add that my students intended no disrespect,
but were simply expressing their immediate reactions, and I
was glad that the second student could speak so candidly.)

Had I omitted the Yozer prayer from the course, I think that my students would have missed something essential to their understanding. However, if they study it, how does one deal with the great gap between the world of the prayer and that of the students?

As I look back at the lectures I gave during the first semester of my teaching, I notice a shift in the way I interpreted Judaism. While arguing for the validity of symbolic expression and historical particularity, and trying to present traditional Judaism in its own language (or the "essence" of its language), my interpretations began to become more abstract and conceptual. I introduced naturalistic, abstract statements from Maimonides, and broad structural reformulations from the Qabbalah, which I clearly labeled as interpretations. For example, after first presenting Jewish eschatology in the form of future history told through somewhat traditional language, during which the students waited patiently for the end, I then added the Lurianic reformulation in terms of the fragmentation and reunification of existence, and then I saw heads nodding with "understanding" and perhaps also with relief at having discovered a meaning to this peculiar account of human destiny. With this kind of encouragement from my audience, I continued to interpret allegorically and conceptually, and to give greater attention to the aspects of Judaism that attracted the students. Moreover, I had already from the start been pointing to areas of experience that Jews and Thai Buddhists might share in common, trying to use this as an interpretative bridge, although I made mistakes guessing about my students' experience. Thus, the image of Judaism that gradually emerged from these interpretations was a rather rationalistic, abstract, and universal one, playing down the miraculous and particularistic, and playing up the ethical. In short, the Judaism of my interpretations (though not the texts I used) verged toward early twentieth-century Reform Judaism, which indeed shared important values with the "Reform Buddhist worldview" of my students.

In the second semester, in the course on Comparative Topics, I attempted a more fundamental and direct interpretation of Judaism, seeking to present it through categories that made more sense to the students while trying at the same time to ground it in classical and traditional texts. I analyzed the biblical and rabbinic images of human nature (just as Buddhist teachers begin with the problems of human nature) and then proposed that Torah (as halakhah) and prayer comprised a path of salvation comparable to, though obviously not the same as, the Buddhist path of discipline, purification, and insight. The Jewish path, I further suggested, leads its followers toward the right relationship with God and society, an ontological and social/moral "fulfillment," as envisioned by Jewish tradition. This experiment produced an interesting and possibly more meaningful picture of Judaism, but one which resulted in the removal from life (again) of the power and redemptive action of God.[28]

Many of my reactions to my situation teaching in Thailand were personal and idiosyncratic; I mention them nevertheless in hope that they may bear some allegorization or application for others (or at least serve as texts to someone's sermon). I began sometimes to think of my teaching as a battle with the students, a struggle for power (and after all, interpretation and understanding do involve power: Whose interpretation prevails and what are the practical consequences? What does an interpretation do to the subject interpreted? What happens to that subject when it becomes part of someone's "knowledge," someone's "comparison of religions"?) I felt isolated during my first year: nearly all my acquaintances were Thai, and the most important people in my life then were my students. The Thai were the majority; I was trying to discover ways of living among them and participating in their life while also meeting my own sometimes different needs. My Californian habits appeared to them, and made me feel by comparison, rather coarse and self-centered. My friends were proud of their culture and wanted me to enjoy it too. In addition, I was the first Jew whom most of my friends and students had met; as I saw my behavior becoming the basis for judgments about Jews in general, I felt compelled reluctantly to behave with those judgments in mind. Then, with my students, I had the impression of everything they heard or read about Judaism being fitted into their own pre-given words, perceptions, values, and thoughts, so that Judaism was blunted and neutralized, was assimilated to Buddhist concepts and Thai cultural forms, relegated to Brahman "superstition," or explained away by categories such as faith, the supernatural, or family loyalty. The students seemed to me to feel certain of what Judaism meant, and I felt equally certain that Judaism was something different. I kept looking for ways to push past what seemed like deflective barriers so that this alien religion could enter and be known, make sense, be respected for itself. (Was I confusing the religion with myself?) While I felt frustrated at meeting repeatedly with locked gates, I continued nevertheless to feel drawn to the company of such gentle, charming, and good-humored gate keepers. To a certain extent, I felt the inferior one in the relationship with my students: it was I who had to explain to them, and it was their response that was important. On the other hand, I seemed myself to be acting like the superior, thinking I was the one who "understood" Judaism, and they the ones who must work to understand and interpret; their mistakes confirmed me in my higher position. I owned the system, empowered by the knowledge at my disposal and my Western academic values to referee the students' attempt to penetrate its maze. And had I myself, with all my reading and listening, and my own analyzing and sorting out, ever penetrated very far into the religion of my students or of their greatest teachers?

I should like now to conclude with a few reflections about the endeavor in general of trying to understand the religions of others. Specifically, my reflections deal with the one region or moment of understanding that I noticed most while in Thailand: the stage in which we tend to perceive the foreign through forms familiar to us in our own experience, probably a universal and even necessary first response to the foreign. Seen from this perspective, looking across cultures, a basic problematic or dialectic arises in I think all attempts to "understand" the other. I hope that my comments may carry some relevance to other students of religion, even though they define the manner and goals of understanding differently than I do. Understanding, one of the most fundamental categories in the study of religions as well as in religious life itself, has been the subject of much discussion and many definitions, although in any form it will always remain something of a mystery, like revelation and enlightenment. Here I want only to speak casually about what impressed me in this one practical situation in which a group of Thai students attempted to "understand" Judaism.

Many of my students, as they readily tell me, were never able to imagine the existence and action of God in the form described by the traditional prayerbook. Mrs. Nanta, for example, told me that she could understnad Judaism only through her own ideas as a Buddhist and a Thai. Thus, as the reader may recall, she thought that the experience of God must resemble her own experience of Kamma. Likewise, when she

heard about the election of Israel and the yearning of Jews
for Zion, she thought that God was also the name that Jews
give to their feelings of love for family, people, and
homeland, and she meant to imply not the slightest disapproval
by this. Other students saw God as an infinitely magnified
thewada, as a consciousness of the laws of goodness and
reality that are Dhamma, as astrological fate, a social
construct for enforcing order, kamma, and so forth. Judaism
as a whole was in this way sorted into the concepts of kamma,
merit, purification, taking refuge, showing reverence, and
precepts, or it was relegated to the realm of the saksit, or
explained away as "faith" and "superstition." I spoke earlier
of my impression that the students were taking everything they
learned about Judaism and remolding it into what they already
knew or felt, or were fittng it into their previously held
explanation of the world. (I again must state that I am
exaggerating somewhat and omitting individual differences
among the students, and that I mean no criticism by this. I
myself was involved as co-conspirator. Rather, I see their
reactions as an allegory for what most of us do when first
confronted with the foreign.) I do not claim that these
translations of Judaism into Thai forms are entirely devoid of
insight; some of the comparisons, as with saksit forms and
with kamma, merit further examination. But I do question
whether such translations deserve to be called
"understanding," because at the very least understanding of a
foreign religion must be understanding of something "out
there," outside the student's own cultural and personal world,
outside what the student knew before she or he tried to
understand. I am reminded of the way that Buddhist
terminology was first translated into Chinese: Dharma became
the Tao, Nirvana became wu-wei (non-action), and sila
(precepts) became hsiao-hsun (filial submission).[29] The
foreign had thereby lost much of its distinction from the
familiar.

Yet on the other hand, it seems to me, understanding must
also be personal in some way. The foreign religion must "make
sense," reveal meaning, to the student in her or his own
world, even as the student disagrees with that meaning. I do
not know how anyone studying a foreign religion could
construct a new mind purified of all associations,
experiences, categories, and language of the culture in which
she or he lives, and even if it were possible, I see no value
in any such self-enclosed, vacuumized perception of a foreign

religion, and especially religion. It leads nowhere. It is cut off from life. That is why understanding must, I think, imply interpretation, connections between "them" and "us," between persons, cultures, histories, and languages.

This, then, is the problematic or dialectic inherent in understanding. Understanding cannot consist in a religion's mere translation into the pre-given forms of another religion and culture (and its sciences and methodologies), cancelling out all distinctions, but understanding also cannot consist in an objectivistic repetition unchanged of what the religion already does in its own foreign language and culture. Or, applied in my situation: if students translate the Jewish experience of chosenness into ancestor worship, or God into astrological fate--they have not understood (or have not done so sufficiently), and if they merely repeat what the prayerbook says, unable to use their own words or connect the subject somehow to their own lives, they still have not understood. Either extreme implies a relationship of the form of Buber's "I-It," with "It" being either a reflection of myself and hence not a relationship with other people, or "It" being a blank object, hanging "out there," meaningless to me. The goal of understanding, therefore, is not so much one of finding a middle ground between two extremes as it is of bringing together two necessary but opposing movements of thought to create a living relationship with the other that leaves the other both distinct from myself and yet alive to myself.

One of my students who seems to have achieved such a relationship with the Yozer prayer is Twan. In a note written to me about the role of nature in revealing God, he connected the prayer with an experience he had had several years earlier while he was an exchange student in California.

> The Prayer that begins with a celebration of God as the creator shows obviously how nature or laws of nature become an indicator for the Jewish people to think of the greatness of God as the creator of all things. The beauty of nature in our world, as once when I was in Yosemite National Park, stimulated me to think about the greatness of the creator even though in my religion there is no God.

Yes, Twan's experience was mostly aesthetic, and the prayer speaks not of nature's beauty but of its orderliness and the divine love and wisdom it shows. And yes, Buddadhadhasa taught his students, Twan among them, that the God of the Christians is to be identified with nature or the laws of nature. Such interpretations do indeed alter the prayer while opening it to Twan's life, yet a part of the essential "foreignness" of the prayer nevertheless remains: "even though in my religion there is no God," nor creation, nor perhaps even "beauty of nature in our world."

Apparently, as Michael Novak suggests, and other scholars before him, we, as students trying to understand a foreign religion, must undergo something of a conversion ourselves.[30] Before this, the religion has no meaning to us: living as we do in a foreign culture, we lack the experiences needed to understand the religion in its given form, and no analogy can fill the gap. Moreover, our habits of thought deflect or cancel out anything important which foreign people might be saying to us. Hence, for an understanding to occur, there must be change. We as students must actively seek meaning in the religion, partly by allowing our experiences to be given foreign meanings, by separating ourselves a little from the explanations and cultural forms that block out the foreign. The "conversion" consists in this change whereby we somehow make room for the other, turning toward the other, allowing our experiences to be restructured, at least provisionally. But in this, too, an opposing consideration arises: our new perceptions must at the same time remain grounded in what we consider real and important, retaining a connection with our life in our own immediate world.

Related oppositions in the endeavor to understand arise from the nature of Judaism itself, and of every other religion that claims universal validity. Judaism is, on the one hand, a specific historical phenomenon rooted in its own culture and language. (This is not to say that Jewish culture has not itself interacted with other cultures and undergone historical changes.) Kadosh has no precise equivalent in the Thai language. On the other hand, as I have already suggested, Judaism makes universal claims that cross cultural boundaries. The truths declared and righteousness demanded by the Torah are meant to apply as fully in Thailand as anywhere else. Hence, Judaism, while approaching the world through the particular history and experiences of one people, is intended to be interpretable everywhere. Perhaps, therefore, understanding should be conceived not as a tension of opposites, but as a drawing out of the particular into the universal (that is, all other particulars). From this viewpoint, interpretation does not oppose the particular uniqueness of Judaism so much as draw out the consequences for other people which are inherent in it.

Midrash is the characteristic manner in which Jews have drawn out the consequences of Scripture for later periods and changed cultural settings. Deriving from methods of reasoning proper to the application of law, midrash occurs in many cases as an analogy discovered between a specific form of expression in Scripture and a specific situation or cultural phenomenon outside of Scripture. Midrash has always been used within the boundaries of Jewish life; however, since it works on the principle that the particularity of Scriptural expression has universal applicaton, midrash could perhaps serve as a precedent or model, or suggest a structure, for drawing out the implications of Jewish tradition, in all its particularity, for the lives of other peole in all of their cultural particularity. The midrash of my students, though based on as-yet-little knowledge of Jewish tradition, shows that people of a totally foreign culture and religion can discover meaning in Jewish Scripture. (It shows also, of course, how easily words can be emptied of their contextual meanings--but rabbinic midrash does this, too, and with great zest.) The midrash of my students points to the possibility of a more knowledgeable interpretation which might preserve the particularity of the tradition while achieving personal relevancy for people outside the tradition.

We may not feel happy with what other people understand about "our" religion. Especially in my first year, I taught with the aim in mind of promoting a sympathetic understanding of Judaism, "from within," which meant an understanding that reproduced that of the ideal Jew I imagined from the prayerbook. However, if my students' understanding was to be personal, it might also be unsympathetic at times. Has not a student understood something about Judaism when he or she sees in it a faith in the unknowable, a similarity to the realm of the saksit in popular religion, or ethnocentrism expressed as chosenness? I myself have reason to disagree with these interpretations, but I cannot deny that they derive from real knowledge seen from a viewpoint different from my own. As Professor Kees Bolle pointed out to me, distaste for certain religious forms may lead to insight into aspects of them which their proponents do not see.

Thus, there are degrees and kinds of understanding. Yet, though this makes another's understanding more difficult to judge, it does not invalidate my argument that transcultural understanding must preserve the subject's foreignness while achieving a personal relevance for the person or society seeking to understand.

NOTES TO "TEXTUALISM/LITERARY THEORY"

Silberstein

[1]See Karl Popper, Objective Knowledge: An Evolutionary Approach (Oxford: 1972) pp. 71-72, 104, 145-46, 257-61.

[2]The term is borrowed from Van A. Harvey, The Historian and the Believer (New York: 1966), p. 49. Harvey's concept of history as a field-encompassing field is indebted to Steven Toulmin's Uses of Argument (Cambridge: 1958), ch. 1.

[3]Useful descriptions of this school of thought are Terry Eagelton, Literary Theory: An Introduciton (Minneapolis: 1983), Christopher Norris, Deconstruction: Theory and Practice (London and New York: 1982), Vincent R. Leitch, Deconstructive Criticism: An Advanced Introduction (New York: 1983) and Jonathan Culler, On Deconstruction (Ithaca: 1982). Culler's work is an advanced and highly lucid discussion of the theoretical issues involved in deconstructive literary criticism.

[4]Philosophy and the Mirror of Nature (Princeton: 1979); Consequences of Pragmatism (Minneapolis: 1982).

[5]In his preface to Sabbetai Zevi (Princeton: 1973), p. xi, Gershom Scholem wrote: "I do not hold to the opinion of those (and there are indeed many of themn) who view the events of Jewish history from a fixed dogmatic standpoint and who know exactly whether some phenomenon or another is 'Jewish' or not. Nor am I a follower of that school which proceeds on the assumption that there is a well-defined and unvarying 'essence' of Judaism, especially not where the evalution of historical events of the past." Scholem refers to his own anarchistic tendencies in an interview reprinted in On Jews and Judaism in Crisis (New York: 1976), pp. 32-33. In the light of his pluralism, his criticisms of Buber's conception of Judaism expressed in the same volume, pp. 126-171, are puzzling.
Louis Jacobs, in the article "Judaism" published in the Encyclopedia Judaica, criticized efforts to speak of a normative Judaism, indicating that "no criteria are available for distinguishing the essential from the ephemeral" (Vol. 10, p. 386). However, in the very next paragraph, Jacobs engaged in a somewhat strained effort to preserve the idea of continuity.

[6]See Scholem, "Martin Buber's Interpretation of Hasidism" in The Messianic Idea in Judaism (New York: 1971), pp. 227-250; and Rivkah Schatz-Uffenheimer, "Man's Relation to God and World in Buber's Rendering of the Hasidic Teaching" in The Philosophy of Martin Buber--The Library of Living Philosophers vol. 22, edited by Paul Arthur Schilpp and Maurice Friedman (La Salle, Illinois: 1967), pp. 403-434. Buber's response may be found in the same volume, pp. 731-741, and in "Interpreting Hasidism, Commentary, 36, 3 (September, 1963), pp. 218-225.

[7]For the concept of structure referring to the fact that all readers approach a text with preconceived categories and frameworks, see Roland Barthes, S/Z, translated by Richard Miller, preface by Richard Howard (New York: 1974), pp. 10-11, and the comments by Jonathan Culler in Roland Barthes (New York: 1983), pp. 78-90. Harold Bloom discusses the issue of canon in Kaballah and Criticism, pp. 95-106.

[8]For an explanation of these terms see below, and notes 10 and 11.

[9]In his response to Scholem, Buber challenged the privileging of the objectivist, historical mode of interpretation, arguing in favor of a mythic mode which seeks to "recapture a sense of the power that once gave it the capacity to take hold of and vitalize the life of diverse classes of people. Such an approach derives from the desire to convey to our own time the force of a former life of faith and to help our age renew its ruptured bond with the absolute" (p. 218). In his early writings on Hasidism, Buber stated clearly that he was not engaging in historical inquiry, and that his work fits into the tradition of myth. See Legends of the Baal Shem (New York: 1969), pp.7-14, especially pp. 10-11: "But my object is not the recreation of this atmosphere. My narration stands on the earth of Jewish myth, and the heaven of Jewish myth is over it."

[10]Bloom uses the term poet to refer not only to those who write poetry, but to all creative writers. See Poetry and Repression (New Haven and London: 1976), p. 2.

[11]The case of intertextuality is effectively argued by Culler, The Pursuit of Signs: Semiotics, Literature, Deconstruction (Ithaca, New York: 1981), see especially pp. 38 and 110-114. See also Leitch, Deconstructive Criticism, ch. 6.

[12]On the concept of "misreading" see Culler, On Deconstruction, pp. 175-179. Harold Bloom develops the concept of misreading in a different directon for which he is indebted to Freud and Nietzsche in Kaballah and Criticism (New York: 1975), especially pp. 95-126, and in The Anxiety of Influence (New York: 1973).

[13]See Rorty, Philosophy and the Mirror of Nature, pp. 365-372.

[14]For applicaton of Kuhn's concept of paradigm to various disciplines in the humanities and social sciences see, Paradigms and Revolutions: Applications and Appraisals of Thomas Kuhn's Philosophy of Science, edited by Gary Gutting (Notre Dame, Indiana: 1980).

[15]The argument against anarchism and in support of the determinacy of meaning is made by E. D. Hirsch, Validity in Interpretation (New Haven: 1967); see also M. H. Abrams, "The Deconstrtuctive Angel" in Critical Inquiry, 3, (Spring, 1977), pp. 425-438. For critiques of the position advocated by Hirsch and Abrams see J. Hillis Miller, "The Critic as Host," in the same issue of Critical Inquiry, 3, pp. 439-447, and "Tradition and Difference" in Diacritics, 2, (Winter, 1972), pp. 6-13; see also, Robert Crossman, "Do Readers Make Meaning?" in The Reader in the Text, edited by Susan R. Suleiman and Inge Crossman (Princeton: 1980), pp. 149-164.

NOTES TO "MY TEXT, YOUR TEXT, OUR TEXT"

Cutter

[1]Neil Postman, Teaching as a Conserving Activity. A summary of Postman's position can be seen in his article "The Day Our Children Disappeared," Phi Delta Kappa, (January, 1981). Two issues of Daedalus underscore the passion and the

range connected with these questions: the Fall, 1982 issue,
"Print Culture and Video Culture," and the Winter, 1983 issue,
"Reading Old and New."

[2]Some individuals with whom I have discussed this
polarity have insisted that the interpretive tradition "PRDS"
(peshat, remez, derash and sod) implies a tolerance for
indeterminacy. But PRDS actually means something else, and
addresses a different kind of problem. The four ways of
looking at Torah implied by PRDS have to do with layers of
meanings, each of which is determinate. In any event, this
article will deal litle with this question, and later work
should.
Actually there are three sets of problems attached to the
question of indeterminancy/normative reading/ and literary
criticism. There is the tradition of normative reading, in
which rabbinic literature, for example, is seen to reflect a
more or less unfied and coherent value system. This tradition
is sometimes countered by a view which may take a given text
as stable, univocal and determinate but insist that it is only
one of many normative texts. Then, there is the question of
whether any text has stability or determinancy in light of the
potential for texts to have multiple meanings. This view is
countered by strenuous efforts to place limits on
interpretation. The third set of problems, which actually
grows out of the second debate, is the extent to which
contemporary canons of literary interpretation from the
secular field should be used to deal with classical religious
material.

[3]See my article, "Reading for Ethics", Journal of Reform
Judaism, 30, (Spring, 1983). The current discussions of the
positive aspects of this perspective occur among critics who
work in the area broadly labelled "reader-response
criticism". Two anthologies can be helpful for understanding
this area: Suleiman and Crossman, editors, The Reader in the
Text (Princeton: 1980) and Jane P. Tompkins, Reader Response
Criticism (Baltimore: 1980). A helpful brief statement about
the possibilities of latent meanings in Jewish texts can be
found in Eugene Mihaly, "The Passover Haggadah as Paradise",
CCAR Journal, 13, (April, 1966).

[4]One of the best known summaries of the question of
genre is contained in Rene Wellek and Austin Warren, Theory of
Literature, (New York: 1948). An issue of New Literary
History, 13, (Autumn, 1981), is devoted to the question of
convention. My personal experience with watching young people
in museums, and working with them on understanding "genre"
comes from the MUSE program of the Hebrew Union College, a
museum education project originally funded by the NEH, and
currently operated as part of HUC's museum and School of
Educaion.

[5]The entire story, in my translation, is as follows:
...And there is a mountain, and on the mountain a stone
stands, and a fountain flows from the stone. Everything has a
heart, even the world has a heart. This heart of the world
has full stature with a face and hands and feet and so forth.
And this mountain with the stone and fountain stands at one
end of the world, and this heart of the world stands at the
other end of the world. And the heart stands opposite and at
great length from the fountain, and longs and throbs intensely
to come to the fountain with great, great longing, and it
cries out to come to the fountain. And the fountain longs for
the heart. And the heart has two weaknesses: one is that the
sun pursues it and burns it because it longs and want to draw
near to the fountain, and the second weakness of the heart is

the extent of the longing and the yearning with which it
wishes to consumate with the fountain, and so it cries; and it
stands opposite the fountain and it cries: Gevalt!! And it
longs exceedingly. And when it needs to rest a bit, so that
it can breathe more easily, a great bird comes and spreads her
wings over it and protects it from the sun, so that it stands
at rest. And when it is resting, it looks at the fountain and
longs for it again. So, why doesn't it grow near the fountain
if it misses it so much? Because when it wants to begin
drawing near to th mountain, then it cannot see the plateau,
and cannot look at the fountain, and when it can't see the
fountain, it dies, because the essence of its life is the
seeing of the fountain.....

In my parallel of the text reading experience to the
parable of the heart of the world and the fountain, it should
be noted that the fountain also longs for the heart. The more
radical text criticism of our contemporary period would be
quite comfortable with the notion that the text takes its
meaning from the reader.

[6]Geoffrey H. Hartman, Criticism in the Wilderness (New
Haven: 1980), part II; Harold Bloom, Poetry and Repression
(New Haven: 1976); and The Anxiety of Influence: A Theory of
Poetry (New York: 1973).

[7]Roland Barthes, S/Z, translated by Richard Miller (New
York: 1974).

[8]Georges Poulet, "The Phenomenology of Reading" New
Literary History, 1, (October, 1969).

[9]E. D. Hirsch, "Objective Interpretation," PMLA, 75,
(1960), pp. 463-79.

[10]Jerome S. Bruner, Toward a Theory of Instruction (New
York: 1966). Bruner, in this work and in his The Process of
Education, presents curriculum materials which grow out of
conferences with scholars and educators who try to identify
the linkage between the front edge of information and
curriculum/teaching methods. The work of Joseph Schwab in the
natural sciences, and I. A. Richards in literature and
metaphysics demonstrates the potential of the relationship
between the scholar and the educational designer.

[11]The "New Criticism" became important in the late 30's
and 40's as a reaction to viewing literature exclusively in
terms of its social utility. Many of its early leaders were
inclined towards an aristocratic and even agrarian attitude
about the industrial north of the United States. Proponents
were Cleanth Brooks, John Crowe Ransom, Ivor Winters, Robert
Penn Waren, and Monroe Beardsley. The New Criticism devoted
itself to focusing on literary texts in more "formalist" ways,
and with concern principally for the relations of elements of
a text to each other. Some of this activity was described by
M.H. Abrams as "Objective Criticism". The New Criticism seems
to have had the effect of reclaiming the value of the text as
a thing in itself; and many of the essays of new critical
writers bear re-reading by educators who tend to view literary
materials in terms of concern with moral suasion.

[12]Norman Holland, 5 Readers Reading (New Haven: 1975).

[13]E. D. Hirsch, The Aims of Interpretation (Chicago:
1976).

[14]Readers of this paper should enjoy explorations of the nature of reading communities. I recomend, particularly, the work of Stanley Fish, Is There a Text in This Class? (Cambridge, Mass: 1980).

[15]Samuel L. Heilman, Synagogue Life, (Chicago: 1973). Steven Copeland, "Value and Experiences of Reading Aloud in Traditional Jewish Text Learning," Ph. D. dissertation, Harvard University, 1978. Although I will not discuss the implications of "aurality" in this paper, some of the points I make in the body of the work assume the reading aloud of the material.

[16]I have not made distinctions in this paper between theme and meaning; and the exclusion may arguably be a flaw in the discussion. A future paper will take up this distinction.

[17]See William Scott Green, "The Case for Rabbinic Biography". See, especially, Ephraim A. Urbach, HaZal (Jerusalem: 1978), for an anthology from which one may cull a particular sage's approach.
For the purposes of instruction, however, what matters in this meaning of biography is that the reader use a personal connection to grasp a meaning and to develop a personal significance. The activity simply requires the caution that the student not interpret the activity as the creation of actual "biography".

[18]Richard A. Lanham, Literacy and the Survival of Humanism (New Haven: 1983).

[19]Hartman, Criticism in the Wilderness, especially chapter 7.

[20]For a brief statement by Neusner on this theme see "The Talmud as Anthropology," The Annual Samuel Friedland Lecture, Jewish Theological Seminary, 1979.

[21]Some of the ideas in this paragraph were stimulated by Armin Hermode, The Genesis of Secrecy (Cambridge, Mass.: 1979).

[22]This is related to Barthes' notion of "tutor text"; see especially S/Z, chapter IX.

NOTES OF "THE WHITE HOTEL"

Corn

[1]Other novels in this category include John Gardner's October Light, John Barth's Lost in the Funhouse, Mario Vargas Llosa's Aunt Julia and the Scriptwriter, John Irving's The World According to Garp, Thomas Williams, The Hair of Harold Roux, Gilbert Sorrentino's Mulligan Stew, and Flann O'Brien's At Swim-Two-Birds. Among the plays constructed as Russian dolls are Tom Stoppard's The Real Inspector Hound and Rosencrantz and Guildenstern Are Dead and Luigi Pirandello's Six Characters in Search of an Author.

[2]Pearl K. Bell, "Self Seekers," review of The White Hotel, Commentary, 72, (August, 1981), p. 59. Bell believes Thomas's heroine compares unfavorably with Hans Castorp in The Magic Mountain because she is "untouched by political and cultural forces." Lisa may not be as aware of political developments as others of her contemporaries, but it is

106 / Approaches to Modern Judaism

precisely the ordinariness of her talent and intellect that
Thomas plays against in his narrative structure: Lisa need
not be extraordinary in the circumstances of her life for us
to appreciate her human worth. Thomas's technique reveals her
inner life so that we may come gradually to cherish her and
mourn her destructon.

[3]D. M. Thomas, The White Hotel (New York: 1981), p. 5.
Subsequent page references in the text are to this edition.

[4]George Levine, "No Reservations," review of The White
Hotel, New York Review of Books, 28 May 1981, p. 22.

[5]Levine, p. 23.

[6]It may be that Thomas has misjudged our ability and/or
willingness to join what Peter J. Rabinowitz calls the
"narrative audience." See "Truth in Fiction: A Reexamination
of Audiences," Critical Inquiry, 4, (1977), pp. 121-41. This
final part of the novel seems a necessary part of Thomas's
structural schemes, but it raises questions that cannot be
satisfactorily answered. Even if the reader acknowledges that
structural necessity, he or she finishes the novel puzzled and
perhaps somewhat frustrated.

[7]Carole Kessler, review of The White Hotel,
Reconstructionist, 47, (March, 1982), pp. 29-30.

NOTES TO "WINNOWING OF AMERICAN ORTHODOXY"

Gurock

These abbreviatons are used in the following notes:

AH   American Hebrew
AJH   American Jewish History
AJHQ   American Jewish Historical Quarterly
AJYB   American Jewish Year Book
HS   Hebrew Standard
OU   Orthodox Union
PAJHS   Publications of the American Jewish Historical Society

[1]Charles S. Liebman, "Orthodoxy in American Jewish
Life," AJYB, (1965), pp. 34-36. Liebman identified
non-observant Orthodox in the mid-1960's as members of
Orthodox synagogues who showed no commitment to Jewish law,
and he touched on some of the motivations keeping them in the
Orthodox synagogue. Some are attracted by a famous rabbi or
congregation. Others find nostalgic satisfaction in the
old-style synagogue. Still others are unhappy with the
perceived "coldness" of the more liberal services. This paper
discusses the history of this significant contingent of
synagogue-goers.

[2]By 1917, the New York Kehillah estimted that there were
approximatly 730 synagogues in New York City alone, most of
them of the landsmanshaft variety. For a short treatment of
the complex history of the social, cultural and religious role
played by the landsmanshaft synagogue, see Di Yiddishe
Landsmanshaften fun New York (New York: 1938). Even as Jews
broke with the social-religious system which supported the
immigrant synagogue, this continued affinity for the old style
services came to the fore--as we will presently see--in the
form of opposition to innovation within Orthodoxy. Finally,

much has been written both in memoirs and in the scholarly literature about the disaffection of Jews from their traditions as part of the Americanization process. For the best primer on the subject see Moses Rischin's classic, The Promised City (Cambridge: 1963), especially the chapters entitled, "Tradition at Half-Mast" and the "Great Awakening." See also Nathan Glazer's American Judaism (New York: 1957), pp. 60-78.

³On attempts to recreate European conditions on American soil, see Abraham J. Karp, "New York Chooses a Chief Rabbi," PAJHS, 44, (March, 1955), pp. 129-198. See also Jonathan D. Sarna's important translation of Rabbi Moses Weinberger's protest against the demise of traditional behavior, People Walk on their Heads: Moses Weinberger's Jews and Judaism in New York, (New York and London: 1981) and Aaron Rothkoff, "The American Sojourns of the Ridbaz: Religious Problems Within the Immigrant Community," AJHQ, 57, (June, 1968), pp. 555-572.

⁴See Glazer's chapter "Judaism and Jewishness, 1920-1945," pp. 79-106 for the most articulate explanation of that tradition.

⁵Marshall Sklare, Conservative Judaism: An American Religious Movement (New York: 1954), pp. 66-128; Will Herberg, Protestant-Catholic-Jew: An Essay in American Religious Sociology (New York: 1955), pp. 186-195; United Synagogue of America, Report of the 17th Annual Convention May 19-21, 1929, pp. 14-16.

⁶For the best account both of the migration patterns of second generation Jews out of the inner city and towards suburbia in this nation's largest metropolis and of the levels of ethnic group persistence as opposed to assimilation achieved by these Jews, see Deborah Dash Moore, At Home in America: Second Generation New York Jews (New York: 1981).

⁷On the history of the Endeavorers see, Bernard Drachman, The Unfailing Light: Memories of an American Rabbi (New York: 1948), pp. 255ff; HS, October 18, 1904, p. 4; and AH, January 4, 1901, p. 233, January 18, 1901, p. 284, February 8, 1901, p. 379, April 5, 1901, p. 596. On the founding of the Young Israel, see AH, January 10, 1913, p. 303; and HS, January 12, 1913, p. 9. See also Jewish Theological Seminary Student Annual (1914), pp. 5-51 and (1915), pp. 51-52, all quoted from and utilized in Shulamith Berger's "The Early History of the Young Israel Movement," (unpublished typescript seminar paper, YIVO Institute, Fall, 1982). On the organizing of the Institutional Synagogue, see Jeffrey S. Gurock's When Harlem Was Jewish, 1870-1930 (New York: 1979), pp. 135ff.

⁸One of the most imaginative ways in which the Endeavorers and Young Israel met the religious preferences of their prospective members was their emphasis on Sabbath afternoon services as their "key" service of the week, a service often followed by a lecture and/or social activity. The young synagogue leaders recognized that many of their potential communicants worked during the day and could only attend an evening service.

⁹Rothkoff, pp. 561-562; AH September 30, 1904, 516; MS, October 7, 1904, p. 7, as derived from Jenna Weissman Joselit, "What Happened to New York's Jewish Jews," Moses Rischin's The Promised City Revisited," AJH, 73, (December, 1983), 163-172; AH, January 16, 1903, p. 295.

[10]Gilbert Klaperman, The Story of Yeshiva University: The First Jewish University in America (London: 1969); Rothkoff, Bernard Revel: Builder of American Jewish Orthodoxy (Philadelphia: 1972) pp. 43-71; The Rabbi Isaac Elchanan Theological Seminary Register 5685 (1924-25), (New York: 1925).

[11]That each of these issues posed real problems for the American Orthodox synagogues and their rabbis is evidenced by the fact that questions on each of these concerns were submitted by members of the Rabbinical Council of America (the organization of Americanized, English-speaking rabbis, founded in 1935) to their Standards and Rituals Committee or to their Halacha Commission from 1935 through 1950's. See Louis Bernstein, Challenge and Mission: The Emergence of the English Speaking Orthodox Rabbinate (New York: 1982), pp. 39-51 and passim.

[12]OU, April 1943, p. 5; April, 1925, p. 11, for discussions by rabbis in the field of the low level commitment exhibited by their rank and file members. Signficantly, contemporary rabbis outside of New York often contrasted the poverty of their pulpit life with that of the metropolis. The statistics on the number of Orthodox Union synagogues are derived from the listings of member organizations published in its organ, The Orthodox Union, a valuable source for the social and institutional history of inter-war Orthodoxy, published 1933-1946. See specifically OU, July, 1937, p. 2, for its boast of numerical predominance. To be sure, exact figures on the number of congregations affiliated with each denomination are simply not available. However, as far as numbers of congregations are concerned, we have an exact account of the Conservative United Synagogue of America for 1929 in the aforementioned Report of the 17th Annual Convention (1927).

[13]In 1935 the OU noted the calling of a convention of Orthodox synagogues on Long Island (which included Queens) at the Far Rockaway Jewish Center attended by its nineteen member congregations. See OU, October, 1935, p. 7. Statistics on the New York-based Young Israel Movement are derived from a circa 1935 pamphlet, Young Israel: Its Aims and Activities, published by its Natonal Council. In figuring denomination affiliation and strength, note also that a number of 1929 USA congregations appear in the OU as part of the Orthodox group. That means that synagogues either drifted back and forth between movements or held dual affiliation.
This argument clealy differs from the interpretations of Sklare and others who see Conservatism winning out over Orthdoxy in the inter-war period. Conservative Judaism's numerical hegemony began, according to this present study, as a post-World War II phenomenon. Though clearly the Orthodoxy of many Orthodox synagogues may have been watered down during this prior era, that does not mean that Conservatism dominated institutionally. As one contemporary 1940's Orthodox rabbi explained: "It is doubtful whether the conservative synagogue has gained much in an organized way [in his city]." There has been unquestionably an upsurge of conservative sentiment in the very ranks of Orthodox congregatoins. See OU, April 1943, p. 5.

[14]See again the previously noted studies by Sklare and Herberg on the growth of these movements. It is suggested here that the periodization of the rise and "conquest" of American Judaism is a post-World War II phenomenon. I am also emphasizing here the significantly changed attitude towards

liberal Judaism of third and fourth generation Jews as opposed
to that of earlier generations.

[15]The strength-or lack or it- of Orthodoxy in three
cities, Boston, Milwaukee and Providence, is indicated in
Morris Axelrod, Floyd S. Fowler and Arnold Gurin, A Community
Study for Long Range Planning (Boston: 1967); Albert J. Mayer,
Milwaukee Jewish Population Study (Milwaukee: 1967); and
Sidney Goldstein and Calvin Goldscheider, Jewish Americans
(Englewood Cliffs: 1968). See also Harold W. Polsky, "A Study
of Orthodoxy in Milwaukee; Social Characteristics, Beliefs and
Observances," in Sklare, The Jews: Social Characteristics of
an American Group (Glencoe: 1960), pp. 325-335.

[16]Liebman noted a generation ago another dramatic change
in Orthodox synagogues, what we might call the clericalization
of the Young Israel. Most Young Israel synagogues are today
headed by rabbis. In its nascent stage, however, the Young
Israel synagogue was known for its lay leadership. See
Liebman, pp. 58-61.

[17]For a basic history of the growth of the Jewish day
school movement over the last generation, see Alvin I. Schiff,
The Jewish Day School in America (New York: 1966), pp. 48-86.
And for an anthropological study of the backgrounds, attitudes
and social dynamics of the Jews attending these new era
American Orthodox synagogues where talmudic learning has
become increasingly important, see Samuel Heilman, Synagogue
Life: A Study in Symbolic Interaction (Chicago: 1973), and
The People of the Book: Drama, Fellowship and Religion
(Chicago: 1983).
    Rabbi Moses Scherer, president of the Agudath Israel,
summed up best the change in the educational orientation of
Orthodox Jews from inter-war days to today: "When I was a
youngster, it was very possible for someone to be an Orthodox
Jew without continuing [intensive Jewish education] beyond
elementary school...Today it is unthinkable that one can
really be an Orthodox Jew unless he had at least graduated
Yeshiva high school:" William B. Helmreich, "Old Wine in New
Bottles: Advanced Yeshivot in the United States," AJH, 69,
(December, 1979), 243.

[18]Israel Meir Ha-Kohen Kagan, Niddehei Yisrael (Warsaw:
1894), pp. 129-130; quoted in Aaron Rakeffet-Rothkoff, The
Silver Era in American Orthodoxy (Jerusalem and New York:
1981), p. 18.

[19]For interesting biographical, albeit hagiographical,
sketches of the transplanted Yeshiva rabbis who rebuilt
communities in America, see Nisson Wolpin, ed., The Torah
World: A Treasury of Biographical Sketches (New York: 1982).
On the settlement patterns and sociology of Hasidic groups,
see Israel Rubin, Satmar: Island in the City (New York: 1982)
and Solomon Poll, The Hasidic Community of Williamsburg (New
York: 1962). For a thoughtful and comprehensive study of the
sociology and mind-set of the Yeshiva world--most importantly,
the Yeshiva's development and maintenance of its sense of
cultural superiority--see Helmreich, The World of the
Yeshiva: An Intimate Portrait of Orthodox Jewry (New York and
London: 1982), pp. 300-331.

[20]See Helmreich, pp. 220-238, for his important
discussion of college education and the students of the
Yeshiva world. And see pp. 272-275 for a discussion of
economic and demographic patterns within that group.
Interestingly enough, though the new era Orthodox see

themselves as resisting, if not merely unimpressed with, American societal phenomena and change, they have been consciously, or unconsciously, affected by American social patterns. The _eruv_ issue is a case in point. The idea that families, and not just grown men, should go to services is an American religious phenomenon.

NOTES TO "TEACHING JUDAISM IN THAILAND"

Marks

[1]My transliteraton of Thai words follows a hybrid system adapted to the English alphabet, indicating neither tones nor length of vowels. Consonants are transliterated generally in line with Mary Hass' phonetic system used in her Thai-English Students' Dictionary (Palo Alto: 1964); but vowels are written in accord with one of the many systems in practical use in Thailand. Personal names appear in the form used by the individual. Usually, but not always (as in the case of "kusol"), I transliterate according to sound rather than spelling.

[2]I should like to acknowledge by name the students whose words appear in this essay--the students whom I taught first (1980-81): Amnat, Arastum, Nongyao, Parichart, Sriphen, Sumadhya, Twan, and Voradej; and those of my second year (1981): Amporn, Angsana, Chintana, Nanta, Sirirat, Sumonnat. I also discussed various aspects of this essay with students of my third year (1982), to whom I express my gratitude.

[3]Charles Keyes, "Ethnology and Anthropological Interpretation in the Study of Thailand," The Study of Thailand, ed. Eliezer Ayal, Southeast Asia Series No. 54 (Athens, Ohio: 1978), pp. 35-36. B. J. Terwiel briefly compares the Buddhism of the Thai middle-class with that of a farming community in central Thailand, in Monks and Magic (Copenhagen: 1975), pp. 274-75. For further discussion of the reforms of King Mongkut and King Chulalongkorn, see S. J. Tambiah, World Conqueror and World Renouncer (Cambridge: 1976), pp. 200-229 and 405-406, in whic Tambiah identifies as major stands of the reformation "intellectualism" (the devaluation of "superstitious" ritual), "rationalism" (correlating and reconciling Buddhist doctrine with "positve science as advocated by the West"), scriptualism, and euhemerism (including a rejection of the Traiphum); and also A. Thomas Kirsch, "Modernizing Implications of Nineteenth Century Reforms in the Thai Sangha," pp. 57-61, and Frank Reynolds, "Sacral Kingship and National Development: The Case of Thailand," pp. 101-107, in Religion and Legitimation of Power in Thailand, Laos, and Burma, ed. Bardwell Smith (Chambersburgh: 1978). The views expressed by my students, representing in part the Buddhism taught officially in Thai schools, can be understood against the background and as an outcome of this nineteenth-century reformation.

[4]The traditional Theravada Buddhist cosmology is described briefly by Tambiah in Buddhism and the Spirit Cults in North-east Thailand (Cambridge: 1970), pp. 35-42, and by Winston King, A Thousand Lives Away (Oxford: 1964), pp. 87-96. A translation of the Traiphum into English by Frank and Mani Reynolds, entitled The Three Worlds According to King Ruang (Stanford and Bangkok: 1978), has recently come into print.

[5]Contemporary Therevada Buddhist thought on the relationship between Buddhism and Western science is discussed by King, "Theravada Buddhism Encounters Science," Chap. IV of Thousand Lives; by Donald Swearer, "Buddhism and Scientific Thought," Buddhism in Transition (Philadelphia: 1970), pp. 78-87; and by Tambiah (1976), pp. 408-409.

[6]This particular kamma-centered Buddhism of my students may be compared to the "kammatic" Buddhism in Burma described by Melford Spiro in Buddhism and Society (New York: 1970). The religion of my students, however, appears more conceptual, less aligned with what Spiro calls "apotropaic Buddhism," and more concerned to decrease suffering "through dhamma," through a realization of life's impermanence and through contentment and purification of mind.

[7]For texts I condensed and rewrote into simpler English around fifty articles and chapters from introductory texts, and typed all of this plus my lectures for distribution. I taught in English, speaking slowly, repeating key sentences and explaiing difficult vocabulary, and tried to make the students feel comfortable conversing in English despite their mistakes.

[8]In the third and most recent group of my students, Siriwan explained this dictum of Antigonos in this way: "Do God's will carefree about the result", thereby alluding to the value of detachment from the fruits of one's actions.

[9]Twan's idea seems to echo the thought of Buddhadasa, with whom he studied. In Buddhadhamma for Students, Buddhadasa says, also in reference to the Kalama Sutta, "In Buddhism we are taught not to believe anyone, not to believe anything, without having seen clearly for ourselves that it is so" (Bangkok: 1966), p. 15. Relevant also is the following statement of Buddhadasa comparing Buddhism with Christianity: "Buddhism tends to be 'pannadhika,' the path with the wisdom-factor predominant,...Christianity tends to be 'saddhadhika,' the path where trust or faith predominates"; Christianity and Buddhism (Bangkok: 1968), pp. 12-13. This idea seems to be reflected in what Amnat and Sumadhya will say later about the importance of faith in Judaism.

[10]Henry Duméry, Phenomenology and Religion (Los Angeles: 1975), Chap. 2.

[11]The only example from the students' readings that fits this definition of faith came from Abraham J. Heschel, who, in an article entitled "On Prayer," spoke of "my faith that God in His silence still listens to a cry." Prayer for Heschel is an act of praise for a silent God which both is necessitated by and also somehow transcends the horrible evils of the world and our own inability to respond in measure. From Understanding Prayer, ed. Jakob Petuchowski (New York: 1972), pp. 69-83.

[12]The word saksit has one minor, though complicating, meaning which applies only to the grounds of a temple. In this meaning, saksit has the sense of "inviolable," not to be violated by profane actions such as cursing or sexual intercourse. This sense of the word, rather close to the English "sacred" in one of its meanings, could not, however, be the sense in which my students were using the word, since they did not apply it to anything Buddhist. See New Model Thai-English Dictionary, Desk ed., compiled So Sethaputra (Bangkok: 1980), p. 382.

[13]Sriphen's idea of magic seems to be based in part on a definition which I presented as being a prevalent one, namely, the attempt to use supernatural power to affect immediate events in human life. (This is a definition which I myself have come increasingly to question.) The students had also read Yehezkel Kaufman's tendentious characterization of the "pagan cultus" as "fundamentally magical," defining magic with an emphasis upon its "automatic" quality and its source in a realm higher than the gods. "The Biblical Age," Great Ages and Ideas of the Jewish People, ed. Leo Schwarz (New York: 1967), pp. 8-10.

[14]The word saksit (in this form transliterated according to its sound) is spelled fully as saktisitthi. This compound form derives from two very old words, sakti, meaning "power," and sitthi, meaning in this connection "just or valid power," of which the former is distantly related to the Latin sanctus through the Sankskrit sakti, here meaning probably "honor or dignity bestowed by inner or divine power." (For this informaion I rely upon the kind assistance of Acharya Boon Ketutassa and Dr. Supadr Panyadeep, professors of Buddhism at Mahidol University.) Many of the saksit elements of Thai religion originate, like the word itself, from India, but some parts do not, originating instead from indigenous and Chinese traditions. I cannot, however, speak knowledgeably about the historical sources of saksit practices. Chap. 2 of Everyday Life in Thailand (Bangkok: 1979) by Niels Mulder provides an introduction, though a rather scornful one, to the phenomenology and cultus of "the saksit" as it is found in the larger towns of Thailand.

[15]Much of this information about saksit phenomena was provided by Acharya Ratree Maruktat, lecturer in Thai history at Mahidol, who has interviewed numerous people in Bangkok and the central provinces in connection with a reserach project studying religious attitudes. Walapa Wongchalard, an officer of the Ministry of Education, has also lent valuable assistance throughout my discussion of Thai culture in this part of the essay.

[16]At least several students consider saksit practices to be "unbuddhist." Parichart, who spoke pejoratively of "the gods revered in Thailand," also wrote the following remarks: "Doctrinal Buddhism does not teach people to supplicate saksit powers. Since. . . people receive reward and punishment from their own actions, it is not necessary to supplicate spirits. Buddhists should keep the true treasures as their refuge--the Buddha, the Truth, and the Brotherhood of Noble Ones, which offer release from all suffering and give real peace and happiness." This is a clear expression of the Buddhist reformation initiated in the nineteenth century. Cf. the monk cited in Tambiah (1976), p. 428: "No external power can deliver a man."

[17]Religion in Essence and Manifestation (New York: 1963), II, p. 681.

[18]Titbarakh, p. 73, and Atah Kadosh, end of the Kedushah, pp. 85 and 201, Hasiddur Hashalem, trans. Philip Birnbaum (New York: 1949).

[19]Kaddish; yishtabah, 69; El Barukh, 71; Et Shem He'el, 74; Ahavah Rabbah, 75; Kedushah, 85; Elohai Nezor, 95; the Targum paraphrase of Isa 6:3: "holy upon earth: his work of might," 131. In the Bible, God's holiness is often associated

with awesome power, as in Ps. 77:13-14, 99:3, 111:9; or, as in Ex. 19:12-24, Num 4:15-20, and 1 Sam. 6:19, with power to punish those who violate the holiness of objects and places dedicated to him. Even when holiness clearly extends to righteous actions outside the cult, there is often a connecton with God's power to punish the violators and redeem the upholders of his holiness: Lev. 19:14 and 32, Ps. 24:3-5, Isa. 5:15-16, and Amos 2:6-7.

[20]Atah Kidashta, 267; Num. 15:40, p. 77; Magen Avot (MA), 273-75; Kiddushim for Sabbath and Festivals; Havdalah; and the frequent phrase, asher kidshanu bemizvotav, "who sanctified us by his commandments."

[21]Recently I set off a surprisingly lively debate among my students by writing the words "holy life" on the chalkboard (in association with Ex. 19:5-6, mentioning "a holy people," goi kadosh) and asking the students to translate into Thai. The point at issue was whether the word saksit properly translated "holy" in this context, and the obvious problem was that a holy life does not imply the possession of wondrous powers, while it does mean a life lived in obedience to God, who Himself exerts wondrous power. The debate continued even during lunch after the class ended.

[22]For example, in Shomer Goi Kadosh, of the Tahanun, p. 105, the congregation asks God to preserve them so that they may continue to sanctify Him: "Guardian of a holy people. . . let not a holy people perish, who sanctify you with teh threefold sanctification." But also in the Tahanun, the congregation acknowledges that they are unworthy of redemptio and so must plea for God's mercy: their holiness alone will not secure redemption. Sabbath, Torah, and Israel are related to power also in another way, one clearly related to the meaning of saksit: they point to three central acts in sacred history, the creation, revelation, and redemption, all of which involve manifestations of divine power.

[23]Awe: Ex. 15:11; Third Benediction of New Year's Amidah; Et Shem Ha'el, in weekday Shahrit, p. 73. Praise: Kaddish; Kedushah; Ps. 99:9, p. 53; Hakol Yedukha, Shahrit Shabbat, 338; Le'el Asher Shabbat (LAS), 339-41. Joy: intro. to Mikhamokha; MA. Blessings and sanctificatoin: Kaddish; Kedushah; Vetiggaleh, 121; Ps. 145:21, p. 59; LAS. The object of these responses, however, is not exclusively holiness, since holiness usually is not separated distinctly from other characteristics of God.

[24]Solomon Schechter, Some Aspects of Rabbinic Theology (New York: 1909), pp. 199-218. George F. Moore, Judaism (New York: 1927), I, 61, 461; II, 101-111. "Holiness in Rabbinic Literature," editors of Ency. Judaica, in Jewish Values (Jerusalem: 1974), pp. 122-26. For comparison with saksit monks in Thailand, I should like to draw attention also to the many rabbis and holy men to whom rabbinic literature attributed extraordinary powers, such as Honi Hamme'aggel, whose prayers brought rain, Hanina b. Dosa, whose prayers cured illness (Moore, II 235-6), R. Shim'on b. Yohai, who could kill men just by casting his eyes on them (b. Shabb. 34a, Midr. Kohelet Rab. on Ecc. 8:1) and the Babylonian rabbis mentioned in this regard by Jacob Neusner, History of the Jews of Babylonia (Leiden: 1965-70), especially IV, 353-62. Whether the powers exhibited by these men is related to any holiness attributed to them, however, remains to be investigated.

[25]I must add that many Thai do consider Lord Buddha to be saksit, having power to help them, and that they pray (bon ban) to him for direct practical help. The question is whether they would continue to revere him even if they did not want his help.

[26]Mulder concluded, with a certain disdain, that attitudes of devotion and piety are generally absent in relation to saksit power "because relationships are mechanical and thus superficial" (pp. 34-35). I myself, however, cannot help feeling that the people whom I see making a wai as they pass an image or spirit-house, or praying (in the way of bon ban) to saksit beings at temples and especially hospitals, express a serious and sincere reverence for the god or spirit. The relationship does not seem "mechanical" for most of the people I see, although it may not be "deep" (a difficult quality to define).

[27]The Thai Bible uses "borisut" in Ex. 15:11 and 30:11, Lev. 19:1 and 11:45, Isa. 6:3, and all the verses listed in Note 19. The use of borisut in Ex. 15:11 seems especially incongruous in its context. I discovered, however, two exceptions to the use of borisut in translating kadosh--Gen. 2:3, "And he established it [the seventh day] as a borisut-saksit day"; and Ex. 3:5, "The place where you stand is a saksit place." In both cases saksit is used in the minor sense applying to temple grounds: "not to be profaned."

[28]The "path-model" of Judaism left neither room nor role for the independent action of God breaking in upon life to call and to redeem, even before a person has taken the first step upon the path. Halakhah, as its etymology suggests, is in a certain sense a path--but it is a path in response to God, not in search of God, as an analogy with the Buddhist Eightfold Path might imply.

[29]Ben-Ami Scharfstein, et. al., Philosophy East/Philosophy West (New York: 1978), 43-44.

[30]Ascent of the Mountain, Flight of the Dove (New York: 1978). "Religious studies are before all else a conversion in one's experience of life" (p. 12). See also p. 24.

INDEX